Praise for *Becoming Whole*

"*Becoming Whole* is best described as a 'pocket therapist.' By sharing optimistic and compelling patient stories, personal reflections, and practical tools, Dr. Kehr literally becomes our 'Companion Advisor' and provides a highly readable framework for understanding and solving many of the common problems we face throughout our lives. Weaving together self-help, psychotherapy, and medication, this book is a must-read for anyone striving to become whole and to create a more fulfilling life."

—**Harry L. Leider, M.D.,** MBA, chief medical officer
and group vice president of Walgreens

"*Becoming Whole* feels so personal, as if I'm sitting and talking with the doctor in his office. I love the vivid, real cases in which we can find ourselves, the step-by-step tactics to do something, and the songs to go with each lesson. It's an emotional, visual, and auditory feast that adds a tactile hug to complete one's transformation to wholeness. My brain is on fire with new energy about what it means to be human."

—**Scott Halford,** Emmy Award-winning writer and producer,
Wall Street Journal best-selling author of *Activate Your Brain*

"*Becoming Whole* takes a new track in providing insights into the therapeutic process. Instead of it being a psychoanalytic mystery, the process of what the therapist is trying to help the patient accomplish is spelled out explicitly. Cogent case examples are given that further clarify the therapeutic interactions. These are in the setting of a holistic approach that also includes medicines, vitamins, and other adjuncts. Together, these provide an excellent road map toward wellness."

—**Robert M. Post, M.D.,** professor of psychiatry at George Washington School of Medicine, head of the Bipolar Collaborative Network, and former chief of the Biological Psychiatry Branch of the National Institutes of Mental Health (NIMH)

"My family is one of the millions who has a loved one with a mental disorder. *Becoming Whole* gave us game-changing, life-saving strategies that helped all of us. Dr. Kehr, who is as empathetic as he is brilliant, delivers on his promise to be a healing companion. The book is destined to become a classic."

—**Mary LoVerde,** Hall of Fame speaker and author of *I Used to Have a Handle on Life but It Broke*

"*Becoming Whole* is an insightful, accessible, powerful, and revealing self-help guide for therapy in which psychiatrist Bruce Alan Kehr, M.D., artfully uses patient stories to illuminate the challenges we face in untangling our hearts. Because these challenges shape the way we experience ourselves and our lives, *Becoming Whole* is not only a healing companion but a valuable life companion as well."

—**Steve Sidel,** founder and CEO of Mindoula Health

"A renowned thought leader in the field of psychiatry, Dr. Bruce Kehr succeeds in demystifying the most complex challenges we face as humans, offering empathy and understanding as well as thoughtful and practical solutions for building the relationships and lives we deserve. This book belongs on every bed stand to serve as a ready resource as well as a helpful reminder of the hope and possibilities of a future when people care for and take care of the people around them."

—**Denise Brosseau,** author of *Ready to Be a Thought Leader?*

"If you are suffering from the aftereffects of having been bullied, manipulated, controlled, neglected, or abused, then this book is for you. *Becoming Whole* offers innovative strategies to bring the emotional peace you long for. I highly recommend this book."

—**Sam Horn,** author of six award-winning books translated into 17 languages, including *Take the Bully by the Horns* and *Tongue Fu!*, top-rated speaker by INC 500/5000

"*Becoming Whole* is an outstanding book written by an expert in the field of mental and emotional health. Dr. Kehr's empathy and passion for helping patients is channeled into this well-written and thorough self-help guide. *Becoming Whole* teaches the reader how to put oneself into the shoes of the patient and then use that perspective to provide comfort and advice to others. *Becoming Whole* uses patient stories to provide the reader with valuable tools to help others and to live a more fulfilling and pleasurable life."

—**Michael Koffler,** president and CEO of Genomind

BECOMING WHOLE

A HEALING COMPANION
to EASE EMOTIONAL PAIN
AND FIND SELF-LOVE

Bruce Alan Kehr, M.D.

GREENLEAF
BOOK GROUP PRESS

Published by Greenleaf Book Group Press
Austin, Texas
www.gbgpress.com

Distributed by Greenleaf Book Group

For ordering information or special discounts for bulk purchases, please contact Greenleaf Book Group at PO Box 91869, Austin, TX 78709, 512.891.6100.

Design and composition by Greenleaf Book Group
Cover design by Dr. Bruce Kehr and Greenleaf Book Group

Cataloging-in-Publication data is available.

Print ISBN: 978-1-62634-385-6

eBook ISBN: 978-1-62634-400-6

Part of the Tree Neutral® program, which offsets the number of trees consumed in the production and printing of this book by taking proactive steps, such as planting trees in direct proportion to the number of trees used: www.treeneutral.com

TreeNeutral®

Printed in the United States of America on acid-free paper

17 18 19 20 21 22   10 9 8 7 6 5 4 3 2 1

First Edition

To Barbara, Melanie, and Lisa, whose unwavering love and unyielding belief in me continuously nourish my compassion and empathy and provide me the strength to heal . . . and to the many patients who have honored me with their confidence and trust and allowed me the privilege of helping them through their emotionally turbulent times.

CONTENTS

Heal the Mutilating Effects of Trauma and Find Self-Love

Heal Your Future

BEGIN THE JOURNEY: EASE EMOTIONAL PAIN AND FIND SELF-LOVE

Session One

Let's Talk

Opening the door to the waiting room and looking out, I notice that there is someone new sitting on the couch. It's you. You look lost in thought and are clearly in distress. I greet you with a warm smile, and as you look up at me, your eyes reveal both nervousness and the faint shadow of hopeful expectation. A familiar feeling of anticipation arises within me as I escort you back to my office: This moment marks the beginning of a new chapter in your life—one defined by healing—and I feel honored to be a part of your journey. Together, we will begin to untangle your heart and ease the emotional pain that has brought you here in the first place. Eager to hear your story, I ask you the first of many questions: "Tell me, what brings you in today? What has been troubling you?"

Your answers reveal a longing to unburden and a desire to be understood. They also subtly hint at your struggle to understand—truly understand—yourself.

"Tell me," I ask, "How do you feel?"

You came in to feel better, to figure things out. Your life may not make any sense to you at all. Perhaps it never has, or, once upon a time, maybe it did, but now you feel lost—confused. I absorb your emotional pain moment to moment as your wounds are exposed one by one: new wounds that need mending and old ones painfully reopened with the hope that they will finally heal.

As your story slowly unfolds, you allow me to join you in a place deep inside your heart, to listen and learn and help it recover from these wounds. But the human heart is complicated—primitive, filled with dark corners, but with areas of illumination too. It is both settled and restless, satisfied and yearning, joyful and grief-stricken, lustful and inhibited, elated and tortured, fractured and whole. At times, our hearts are at war with others. At times we are at war within ourselves.

Our hearts and minds tend to repeat patterns of feeling and behaving that can sabotage deep emotional intimacy, unintentionally wounding others or ourselves. The triggers may be events in the present that evoke the past through the unconscious,[1] a vast swamp beyond our awareness filled with memories, feelings, and our darkest thoughts, at first dimly perceived. As they become more visible, they may be frightening; we try to avoid them at all cost by establishing an elaborate defensive system that represses[2] the demons inside.

Ridding ourselves of the demons in our hearts can be a terrifying process. We keep them under wraps for good reason: To reawaken them may overwhelm our sense of self and threaten to crush it. Yet they tangle up our lives and sabotage our happiness. It may be painful, difficult, and emotionally challenging, but working through repressed thoughts and memories is the first step toward healing. However, you don't have to face this challenge alone: I will be at your side for as long as it takes. I will be your companion.

Those who enter my office and sit on the couch must muster up their courage to open up in a way that they may never have before. A wise psychiatrist once said, "Never underestimate the power of listening. You may be the first person in their entire life who ever truly listened." For me, this work is both a calling and a privilege. I'm glad you're here. Let's get to work.

What to Expect from this Book

PATIENT STORIES

The contents of this book are devoted to helping you untangle your own heart or the heart of a loved one. Each of the twelve sessions that follow will explore a commonly experienced emotional issue in depth, using patient stories to clarify and contextualize key themes and outcomes. I will discuss these issues as if you were actually in treatment with me and will provide specific guidance to help you feel better, function more effectively, and end the patterns that sabotage your happiness. By walking you through the ways a psychiatrist or psychotherapist can help resolve these issues, I hope to empower you to seek out your own resolutions, whether that means using this book as a self-help tool for your own personal reflection, seeking therapy for the first time, changing your treatment plan, or helping your loved ones find the support they need.

I'll also invite you into my office and share with you the secret inner lives of a number of my patients. Although these stories are fictionalized, they represent how I've helped real people become whole. By reading them, you will learn how talk therapy uncovers a patient's unconscious feelings and memories; how a psychotherapist empathizes, interprets, and clarifies; and how this process untangles the patients' hearts and ends the patterns that sabotage their happiness.[3] Throughout each story, I will share with you some of the healing comments I made to the patient at key inflection points in their therapy, as well as what I was feeling at the time. At other times, I will share with you how they expressed deeply held, intense feelings toward me (called **transference**[4]) and how we were able to use those experiences to further their understanding of other important relationships in their past and present.

What you'll come to appreciate is a portrait of how the patient and I interact and how feelings and memories from my own life emerge to enable me to join the patient where they are. I will share my feelings with you at these crucial moments, as they will deepen your understanding of what goes on inside the mind and heart of a therapist to facilitate the healing process. Each exchange will illuminate a brief interlude in the telling of the tale, where I offer support, clarity, and hopefulness as the therapy unfolds. I want these tales from real therapy sessions to demystify psychiatry, talk therapy, and the healing process itself and to give you an idea of whether this is something you may need in your own life.

A cautionary note: Some of the patients' stories, particularly those that describe a history of childhood sexual abuse, may be particularly disturbing. In reading them, you may feel that they have nothing in common with your own childhood. You may decide to stop reading partway through the story, and if you feel that is best for your emotional well-being, I respect your decision. At the same time, I promise you that each story, no matter how dire or desperate, will end on a hopeful note and will have something to teach.

THE BIOPSYCHOSOCIAL MODEL

At times, self-help is not enough to alleviate emotional suffering. This is where psychotherapy[5] and psychopharmacology[6] can be enormously helpful. Most of the stories in this book relate to patients in talk therapy who are also receiving medication. Although it is not the focus here, I will discuss how to select a psychotherapist or psychiatrist that best meets your needs, the roles of different prescription medications and supplements, and how to work with your doctor to uncover underlying psychological and medical conditions that affect how you think, feel, and function.

The **biopsychosocial model**[7] is a way of understanding how emotional suffering and illness are affected by multiple factors ranging from societal to molecular; **epigenetics**[8] refers to how external factors, including your lifestyle choices, can switch genes on and off inside your brain cells, for better or for worse. Under the biopsychosocial model and using epigenetic principles,[9] a psychiatrist evaluates and treats the **whole person**, not just a series of symptoms. The fundamental principles of this model involve the interplay of biology, early life experiences, and recent and current relationships, which are woven together into a framework of understanding that allows you and your doctor to make sense of what is going on inside and around you, to begin to untangle your life.

Doctors who practice this model look at every relevant domain in your life—including genetic, biological, psychological, family, social, environmental, existential, and spiritual—and seek to understand how these domains work together or against each other to affect your well-being. They thoroughly assess the history of your condition, as well as your family history, and they may suggest genetic testing or other laboratory tests to gain more insight and provide an even deeper and well-informed evaluation.

You should choose a psychiatrist who practices under the biopsychosocial model—one who will leave no stone unturned in getting to the bottom of all of the factors that interfere with your full recovery. Your doctor will partner with you to develop a comprehensive treatment plan to achieve a full remission of your symptoms—to enable you to **become whole**.

MY QUESTIONS, YOUR ANSWERS

I am a physician, attended medical school, and trained at a psychiatric residency program. I have been practicing psychiatry for nearly forty years. My patients have taught me countless lessons every single day about how to heal a human heart that may feel lost, hopelessly conflicted, or in seemingly interminable emotional pain.

You and I will partner together to leverage these lessons as I teach you to untangle your heart. Much of the teaching will be in the form of questions that I pose to you. You will reflect on your life more deeply and will want to develop as comprehensive an understanding of yourself as possible. Then, I will provide clear steps that will help you end the behavioral patterns that sabotage your happiness and that will lead you down a path to a richer life experience. You'll find these steps at the end of the sessions, in a section called "Begin to Heal."

As you answer these questions about yourself and those you love—and some of the questions will require a good deal of hard thinking—you will broaden and deepen your understanding of why your life is tangled up. I strongly encourage you to write out your answers to the questions as you go along in a notebook or journal that I'll refer to throughout as your "workbook." Your workbook will become a valuable asset that you can refer back to from time to time, particularly during periods of emotional distress, to help further your understanding. Writing out your answers will help you think about your situation in a new way, and you may discover a path forward that you hadn't thought of before. If you are not yet in therapy and decide to begin, these answers can also serve as a starting point to help the therapist get to know you and give you an early view of what to expect.

THE ROLE OF MUSIC

I love music, especially for the therapeutic, healing potential it holds. It is a universal means of expressing the human condition. I use it at times in my practice, particularly as a way to reach patients who initially find it difficult to express their emotions. As we begin therapy, they may find it easier to relate to feelings that are poignantly portrayed in the lyrics of certain songs than to relate to me. In addition, music may help a patient access certain emotions and memories that were previously buried in their unconscious mind. I've tried to recreate that experience for you in this book.

Most sessions will feature a popular song that portrays aspects of the human condition illustrated by the patient's story (for links to the songs and other information, visit DrBruceKehr.com/music). The lyrics may relate to your own story as well and may elicit thoughts, feelings, and memories from inside of you. The songs will teach you more about the human heart and will further your capacity to think about yourself and your life.

And it is not just the lyrics themselves. If you also listen to the timbre of the singer's voice, it can move you to feel powerful emotions.[10] You may feel less alone by listening to songs that connect with how you are feeling and what you are struggling with in your own life. You may also be inspired to reach out to a loved one who may have shut you out or who has difficulty identifying and vocalizing their own feelings.

How to Use this Book

Each session contained in this book will bring new insights into patterns of behavior and emotional vulnerabilities that tangle you up. That said, the way you choose to read this book is entirely dependent on what you're hoping to get out of it.

If you are looking for an in-depth overview of what treatment looks like and can achieve, you may choose to read the entire book. It contains many valuable lessons that will bring you a richer understanding of your own life and the lives of those you love. Reading the stories of people overcoming crises will leave you feeling hopeful, inspired, and less alone.

If you are seeking relief from a specific problem, you can use this book in a highly targeted way. Simply consult the table of contents to zero in on the issues that pertain to your current circumstances—the ones that create that feeling of inner turmoil—and before long, you will be on your way to feeling better. You may find yourself consulting the individual chapters of this book again and again as those circumstances change and evolve throughout your life or lending out the book to your loved ones as they work to solve their own issues.

Begin to Heal:
Get Started by Looking Inward

Let's begin the process of untangling your life by introducing you to self-reflection and psychotherapy. Use your workbook to begin journaling your answers. You might want to glance at all the questions before you begin writing, because some of your answers may overlap—and that's okay. If your answers to one or more of these questions make you feel uncomfortable, sad, or angry, that's okay too. Don't rush this process. It could take you a half hour or half a day. There is no right or wrong way to go about addressing these questions; the main goal here is to simply work through all of them.

Step 1: Let's examine how you have been feeling recently.

In general, how has your life been going? Are you basically satisfied in your love relationships? If not, why?

What about relationships at work—how are they going? Are you satisfied with your job or career? Is it consistent with your interests and aptitudes? Write out what you love and what you hate about your work.

Are you able to like and love yourself, recognizing with pride your many strengths, despite your inevitable flaws and shortcomings? If not, how are you feeling about yourself? Do you feel that you are moving forward in your life? Or are you stuck in an unhappy and emotionally painful place? If the latter, list the sources of emotional pain. Do you feel imprisoned by feelings of anger and disappointment? If so, describe how these feelings are affecting you and your life. Do you feel unloved, disliked, or disrespected? If so, by whom?

Are most days a struggle? Or do you generally feel pretty good, able to weather the ups and downs of life? If the former, describe how you feel on those days. Do you feel that control over your life basically resides within you? Or do you feel battered and blown about by forces and circumstances around you? If the latter, describe those forces and circumstances and how they affect your day-to-day life. Is the stress in your life manageable? Or do you frequently feel overwhelmed? If the latter, what are the sources of these feelings?

Step 2: Begin to write the history of your problems.

When did your life begin to go off track? What was the setting? Describe it in as much detail as you can. Who were the people involved? How did they behave toward you? How might you understand their behaviors in the context of what was going on in their life at that time? What life stresses were they living through? What is their relationship like with their mother, their father, and their significant others, and how might that influence their behavior toward you? Was there a major disappointment or heartbreak in your life that you need to grieve? What was it?

Step 3: Engage in the Process of Introspection.

Once you have written out the answers to these questions, read them over several times to let them sink in. Write down any associated thoughts that come to mind. Then meditate on the answers and the questions themselves by engaging in the process of introspection: by dedicating thirty or forty-five minutes a day—perhaps in the evening in a quiet, darkened room—to begin to think about these issues. If this feels overwhelming, shorten the amount of time to five or ten minutes. Talk to yourself about what you are thinking and feeling. An inner dialogue in the service of understanding is a good thing.

Your troubles may relate to something that happened recently at home or at work that you can figure out on your own, by providing yourself sufficient time for reflecting on it. You can also speak with a trusted friend, family member, or partner who can provide support and advice. Recent upsets or traumas, ones that are not too entrenched, sometimes respond well to ventilating and unburdening to a caring and loving person in your life and do not require professional intervention.

Feel Hopeful and Optimistic as We Work Together

Within your own heart, there is a complicated tangle of emotions that continually influence your thinking and behavior. Conscious emotions are but a small portion of those that govern how you think, feel, and behave; they are the tip of the iceberg.[11] If your heart feels all tangled up, by reading this book, you will begin your own personal journey to untangle your heart *and* your life—and to begin becoming whole. It's important that you nourish this hope; the road to emotional health is long and difficult, but it's crucial that you not give up.

You no longer need to feel alone with your emotional distress. I will join you on your journey as our work together unfolds. In the lessons that follow, you will discover that there are many others out in the world just like you, and you will recognize aspects of yourself as you read about them.

If you remain steadfast in your journey, you will uncover the story of your own heart, come to know yourself better, and begin to gain some powerful insights. You will identify patterns of thinking, feeling, and behaving that have needlessly tangled up your life and that have sabotaged your happiness in love and at work.

"Knowing yourself is the beginning of all wisdom." Aristotle's words are as relevant today as during his lifetime, almost 2,400 years ago. They are further supported by a similar quote by Socrates: "The unexamined life is not worth living."

Now that you know what to expect, let's get started.

Let's talk.

SESSION TWO

Entering Therapy: It Takes Courage to Face Yourself

If the sessions contained within this book are unsuccessful in helping you bring about any meaningful change, and you have persisted in implementing what you have learned (there are no quick fixes after all), it may be time to seek out a psychotherapist. We all have unconscious feelings and memories within us that can exert surprisingly great effects over how we think, feel, and behave. In addition, we may have a biological condition that overwhelms our natural coping mechanisms. Or we may find ourselves in a chronically distressing relationship at home or at work. Repetitive behaviors that sabotage your life and tangled situations that just won't go away are reasons to consider seeking outside help.

Two patients recently shared novel perspectives on therapy with me. The first patient—a tough, charismatic, and highly talented college football player—put it like this: "You have to man up and face yourself in therapy." The other patient, a middle-aged professional woman from the financial services industry, described therapy as a place where "you are not a side effect of your life; you are an active participant in your own well-being."

I genuinely admire those who engage in psychotherapy and commit to seeing it through—thereby bringing about personal emotional growth and a more satisfying life. Patients enter therapy for a variety of reasons. Perhaps they want to end a pattern of self-sabotaging behavior that prevents true intimacy with others; maybe they behave in ways that preclude joyful living or repeatedly choose to fall in love with narcissists or find other ways to unconsciously live out what is known as **the repetition compulsion**.[1] They may also be seeking understanding and relief from recurring symptoms of anxiety or depression. A life crisis over the end of a love relationship, the illness or death of a loved one, or severe job stress may lead them to urgently seek therapy, looking for immediate relief.

♪ **Session Soundtrack** ♪

When I think about patients entering therapy for the first time, the Coldplay song "Talk" comes to mind. Individuals often begin to consider seeing a therapist when they feel lost or incomplete or like they're missing a piece of their puzzle.

Visit DrBruceKehr.com/music-1 for audio files
and further discussion of the soundtracks.

Considering therapy for the first time can be a daunting prospect—filled with emotions ranging from fear and anxiety to anticipation and eagerness. You may wonder to yourself, *What will the doctor be like? Will they be kind and understanding or strange and awkward? Will they judge me or think I'm crazy? Will they tell me what to do or help me figure it out for myself? Will I want to run out of that office and never go back? Or will I want to continue, because I feel understood and sup-ported?* It is understandable if you are dreading the initial encounter. On the other hand, perhaps you can't wait to start unburdening yourself and untangling your life. All of these feelings are normal.

What is necessary in making this commitment to therapy, in sitting with a psychotherapist and examining your life? At its core, the psychotherapeutic relationship requires shared courage on the part of the patient and the therapist. We're embarking on this journey together, with no defined roadmap. At the beginning and from time to time during the course of treatment, the experience can feel scary for the patient. Coming to terms with certain previously avoided realities is emotionally challenging and may feel daunting. At times, extremely painful feelings, embarrassing or shameful fantasies, and troubling memories will arise, all demanding the courage to confront, explore, understand, and resolve them.

The foundational elements of a successful therapy include persistence, developing trust, feeling understood and cared about, feeling emotionally "held"[2] through difficult and painful moments, mutual respect, a high level of technical skill on the part of the therapist, and a shared optimism regarding the outcome. The therapist must also exemplify a deeply held belief in the human spirit's capacity for growth and change. Ultimately, it takes heart, and a strong belief in the patient's (and the therapist's own) courage, to forge ahead into the unknown.

The Language of Therapy

If you decide to venture down this "road less traveled" to begin your journey of self-discovery by working with a psychotherapist, one way to feel less frightened is to begin to understand the language of therapy. Below are a few of the most commonly used terms that help explain some important

continued on next page

underlying concepts of the therapeutic process. You will see examples of all of these concepts in action in the patient stories throughout the book.

Resistance[3] stems from defense mechanisms that protect the conscious mind from experiencing emotionally threatening unconscious memories, fantasies, and feelings. Sometimes, resistance is experienced as an urge to run—to avoid facing these issues—because it is human nature to seek pleasure and avoid pain. Internal conflicts also arise over feelings of dependency toward the therapist, in opposition to the desire to remain independent and self-sufficient. This is often manifested by the belief that seeking treatment is "a sign of weakness" and that "I should be able to manage my problems on my own." To the contrary, when you commit to the therapeutic process and see it through to conclusion, it signifies an admirable strength of character.

Transference[4] occurs when a patient transfers conscious and unconscious feelings and fantasies they had toward important figures from their earlier life, such as their parents, onto the therapist. These may include deep feelings of love or a longing to be loved, fearfulness, erotic fantasies, a yearning to be taken care of, and so on. Optimally, transference feelings should be openly discussed in the session, no matter how embarrassing it may feel, so that the underlying issues can be resolved. If the transference feelings are not candidly revealed, the effectiveness of the therapy will grind to a halt.

Countertransference[5] occurs when the patient elicits conscious or unconscious feelings, fantasies, and memories in the therapist derived from their upbringing and from meaningful relationships. It is important that the therapist has engaged in their own personal psychotherapy or psychoanalysis so that they are able to identify and analyze their countertransference reactions (particularly the unconscious ones), so as to not act them out on the patient or contaminate the therapy by imposing their own personal neurotic agenda. My own psychoanalysis has been valuable in helping me more effectively empathize with, support, and heal my own patients.

Free association[6] is a technique that encourages patients to speak whatever comes into their mind, without holding back or censoring their thoughts, fantasies, or feelings. This exercise is especially helpful when analyzing the unconscious causes of self-sabotaging behaviors that often originate in childhood, an important element in longer-term psychoanalytic or psychodynamic therapy.

Abreaction[7] is when the patient reexperiences prior events in their life with great emotional force—at times, so powerful that it may feel like they are actually living through the experience once again at that very moment. This may occur during the process of free association.

Memory reconsolidation[8] is the process that enables previously consolidated emotionally traumatic memories to be reconsolidated or overwritten, such that new learning renders them less traumatic. As a result of the abreactive experiences and the caring and empathy provided by the therapist, the traumatic event may be recast in a new cognitive framework and viewed without distortion through adult eyes, enabling the patient to finally let go of the trauma.

Begin to Heal

The journey of therapy does not come with a roadmap, and at the beginning of treatment, you may feel that not much in your life makes sense anymore, that you keep returning over and over again to the same emotionally stuck place in your heart. You don't know where you're going, and you feel lost or incomplete. Whatever you're feeling, it is important to muster up your courage and enter that first session with a clear idea of what you would like to cover and what you would like to get out of the evaluation and treatment. Write out in advance what you would like to come to understand and which symptoms you would like to relieve. The following steps will help you reflect on this matter. Answer the prompts and questions in your workbook.

Step 1: Identify what you are feeling and begin to help yourself.

You may feel despair or that something is just not right. Do you feel scared or worried about a recent life event? Are you suffering from depressed feelings that just won't go away? Do you experience emotional pain that feels like too much to bear? What are the feelings at those times?

To begin to feel better, I would encourage you to try out the self-help techniques that I introduced in our first session. Additional tools that may pertain to your particular symptoms or life situation can be found in later sessions. A patient and diligent pursuit of these methods may be enough to begin to turn your life around.

Step 2: Begin to identify patterns that sabotage your happiness, and search for some of the root causes in your childhood.

Do you keep repeating self-sabotaging patterns of thinking, feeling, or behaving? Describe them.

Have you persistently pursued some of the introspective techniques that we discussed in session 1? What are your results so far? What have you been unable to solve through introspection?

Have you spoken with a friend or family member to seek

emotional support and a sounding board to figure out what is going on with you? Did this help? If so, how? Have these talks helped for a while but don't result in any lasting benefit? What happens? Despite outside support, do you feel increasingly depressed? Describe your mood.

Do you have excessive anxiety? Where do you feel it? What are the triggers? Are you suffering from continuing insomnia? Is it trouble falling asleep? Staying asleep? Waking up early in the morning? All of the above?

Step 3: Explore entering psychotherapy.

Do your symptoms persist or worsen, despite efforts to help yourself? If so, it is time to consider entering therapy.

Do you have persisting thoughts or feelings that you might be better off dead? Please describe them. If you feel unsafe, it is imperative that you seek professional help as soon as possible.

Psychotherapy is devoted to helping you feel better, function more effectively, and examine yourself and your life in a new way that will liberate you from emotional restraints, from the shackles that have held you back for years. What are some of these shackles? List them.

Do you resist taking that first step to pick up the telephone and book that first appointment? Please write out some of the reasons.

Although you may feel afraid to start therapy, deep inside you is an awareness that you need a new approach to solving your emotional problems. The old ways of managing and coping just aren't working anymore, and without a new approach you will remain stuck in a very painful emotional state.

Step 4: Are you resistant to entering therapy? Here are some commonly held fears.

Are you afraid that the therapist and the experience will be weird? Please describe what you picture.

Do you feel that once you start talking, you will never want to stop (because what you are wrestling with feels so overwhelming)?

Do you fear there is no hope for you? If so, why?

Did a friend or family member engage in therapy and have a bad experience or never get better? What happened to them? Might they have been responsible for a bad outcome? If so, how?

Do you have conscious or unconscious fears that the therapist will be judgmental? What do you believe they will criticize?

Are you concerned that the therapy will make you feel worse? Please describe why.

Do you believe that the therapist will not understand, will give bad advice, or urge you to break off an important relationship? What specific concerns make you feel anxious in this regard?

By writing out these fears and considering each of them, I hope that you will be able to put them to rest. All of these fears are unfounded if you select the right therapist.

Step 5: How to select a good therapist.

Seek out a psychiatrist, therapist, or a leader at your church or temple (if you prefer a faith dimension) with a strong reputation for being caring, effective, and ethical. Ask your doctor or other trusted healthcare professional for a recommendation. If a particular name is mentioned more than once, that's a good sign. Check online for information regarding their education, background, and what other patients have said about them. Have they won any prestigious awards? Have they been cited for any ethical sanctions or malpractice actions?

Is it possible to have an introductory phone call? If so, prepare your questions in advance. Begin the call with a brief overview of why you are seeking help and what you wish to accomplish in treatment. Then, ask them the following questions:

- What is your treatment philosophy?

- What will take place in the first session?

- If I need medication, is it something that you would prescribe, or will you refer me to someone else? If you refer me, how do you coordinate my care with them?

- Will I be comprehensively evaluated and treated as a whole person under the biopsychosocial model, and what should I expect?

- What is your experience in evaluating and treating patients like me?

- Based on what I have told you so far, is it possible to estimate the length of time that I will need treatment?

- What are your fees? What is your cancellation policy?

The goal of the introductory phone call is to help you decide whether it makes sense to schedule that first appointment—to make a preliminary determination as to the likelihood of a good fit between you and the psychiatrist or therapist. Of course, there is no substitute for a face-to-face meeting to help you decide whether you like them or whether you should keep looking. Do your research, pick up the phone, and place this most important call to begin to untangle your heart.

Select someone who facilitates, helps you figure out what is right for you, and doesn't simply tell you what to do. In therapy, it is mainly your job to figure out your thoughts, feelings, and decisions—not the therapist's—so you don't need to worry about being controlled or dominated. The therapist is there to help you untangle your life, not to mold you into their image. Ultimately, you should thoughtfully evaluate any comments made by the psychiatrist or therapist to see if they make sense. You will accept some comments and reject others. *You* are in control of the therapy and your life, not the therapist.

What matters most is your belief that there is a good fit between the two of you. Do you develop a warm rapport with one another in the first few sessions? Do you feel understood? Is the therapist emotionally supportive and nonjudgmental? Do you feel genuinely cared about? Do you like them? Do you feel that they like you? Are you gaining insight and starting to feel better after a few sessions? And most important of all, over time, as the relationship develops, do you come to feel emotionally safe with them? If the answer to most of these questions is yes, then you have made a good choice and are on your way to deeper understanding and symptom relief.

If the answers are mostly no, find someone else to treat you.

If you feel that you and the therapist may be a good fit but feel disappointed after the first few sessions, express your disappointment directly to the therapist. This accomplishes two important objectives: First, both of you are clear on the goals you wish to achieve. Second, you begin to assertively take charge of your life to achieve what you want, thereby using the therapeutic relationship as a laboratory for behavior change in other important relationships in your life.

Step 6: Have the courage to persist in therapy.

It takes courage to continue in ongoing therapy. Fantasies, memories, feelings, and hidden aspects of oneself begin to surface, which may be frightening or emotionally threatening.

At times, a deeply held unconscious memory of a traumatic

experience may be on the verge of surfacing into your consciousness, and this may bring feelings of high anxiety or even panic. It is important that you let your therapist know what you are feeling at these times and that you ask for additional emotional support. Their empathetic care can help you face what feels so intimidating and overwhelming. Have confidence that you can work through any issue, to feel better and lighter.

The love and support of a friend or family member can prove invaluable after a particularly rough session. You may recall courageous family members who faced seemingly insurmountable odds and overcame many obstacles. Draw strength from their tenacity. Even actively remembering a loving relationship from childhood to hold inside yourself can help you stick with it when the going gets tough by recalling and thinking about times you felt loved and supported by someone. Look at old pictures of those who loved you to evoke memories that may be sustaining.

The unconditional love and comforting presence of a pet can help you feel more supported. Try to remember a loving pet from childhood; children often talk with their pets at times of emotional distress, and memories like this can provide solace.

And finally, a caring, empathetic, and nurturing therapeutic relationship can strengthen your resolve. Permission to call your therapist after hours or arranging for an extra session when you feel overwhelmed will also help you stay the course.

Continue in therapy until you have accomplished your goals for treatment, and when you feel ready to end your treatment, discuss your reasons with your therapist. Determine whether the two of you agree that it is time to end. Your therapist may feel that there are additional issues to resolve, and although you may initially disagree with their assessment, explore the reasons for their opinion in more detail prior to unilaterally terminating the therapy. Early withdrawal may be associated with a number of negative outcomes.[9]

It is imperative that you not give up, that you not run away. Ultimately, you will develop a deep sense of pride in facing your problems, as opposed to denying or avoiding them. Acting courageously to face the painful, shameful, regret-filled, humiliating aspects of your life will ultimately bring you greater self-respect, self-regard, and the freedom to live more fully. Your return on this investment will be exponential.

This may have been an intense session for you. Next, we will discuss how psychotherapy can help you take control of your life or help your children take control of theirs. Let's learn how.

HEAL YOUR
CHILD'S HEART—
AND YOUR OWN

Session Three

Take Responsibility for Your Life, at Any Age

My family went through some hard times during my childhood. In 1959, my mother almost died following complications that developed during a routine surgical procedure. As a result, she developed a deep depression and had a prolonged recovery period. In 1961, my father lost his printing business and had to file for bankruptcy. Money was so tight that we bought our clothes from a second-hand clothing store, and we lived in constant fear of losing our home to foreclosure. My father was a man of integrity, honor, and responsibility, and he dealt with his reality head on. Throughout bankruptcy, he knew that our economic survival depended on all of the will, energy, tenacity, and drive he could muster. He had a tremendous work ethic and labored continuously day and night for three years, brokering sales between former customers and competitors until he finally restarted his business.

My father's strength and virtue carried us through these difficult times fraught with emotional pain and humiliation. He gave me a childhood where I learned that difficulties could be overcome through hard work, self-discipline, and the ongoing encouragement of a parent who never gave up on teaching his value system to his son and living it out personally. Most important, he taught me that I had to take responsibility for my own life, that I wasn't entitled to anything; had to learn to behave in ways that advanced my independence; and, as a result, would develop self-respect. His insistence that each of us take personal responsibility for our lives is a value that I carried with me into my career.

In fact, this value is a cornerstone of psychotherapy. After I became a psychiatrist, I had the good fortune of serving as the medical director of adolescent, mixed adolescent and adult, and neuropsychiatric inpatient units at a private psychiatric hospital. We treated seriously ill patients with severe schizophrenia and bipolar disorder, not uncommonly suffering from substance abuse disorders as well. On one unit, a number of patients had also sustained brain injuries. There was one clearly articulated, overarching rule for each of the patients on those units, regardless of how sick they were: "You are responsible for your behavior."

Every patient had to take personal responsibility; we gave them no other choice. Nobody would be allowed to blame the staff, doctors, medications, or other patients for their behaviors. It was remarkable how infrequently the patients behaved aggressively on these units, given the severity of their illnesses, and how reassured the patients felt in realizing that each of them would be held accountable for how they treated other patients and staff.

Perhaps there is someone in your life—a child, other family member, or a friend—who suffers from feelings of entitlement and who refuses to take responsibility for their life. How is that working for them? If you are really honest with yourself, you may have a streak of entitlement within you as well. How is this attitude working out for you? How does it relate to feelings of self-esteem and self-respect?

As Ayn Rand once noted, "You can avoid reality, but you cannot avoid the consequences of avoiding reality." In psychotherapy, one is forced to confront reality, both within the unconscious mind and in family and work life. The decisions made and actions taken by you will determine your outcome in life. Only by taking full responsibility will you be able to grow as a person and fully experience the richness that life has to offer. In this session, we will discuss the relationship-destroying effects of entitlement at various stages of adult life and the personal growth that can occur through holding yourself accountable for your own behavior. I will also describe how you, as a parent, can impart these values to your children.

> ♪ **Session Soundtrack** ♪
>
> Some of the themes of this session are captured in the song "It's My Life" by The Animals. The lyrics describe a man who feels entitled to take from women by lying and squeezing them dry to live off their money. A man who wants to take all he can get, the narrator feels entitled because he feels it's too hard to get a break, and because "all of the good things" are already taken. He thinks he therefore has the right to steal from others and manipulate them to feed his wants and desires. He takes no responsibility for his life. The world is the problem, not him. Have you had destructive feelings like this?
>
> Visit DrBruceKehr.com/music-2 for audio files
> and further discussion of the soundtracks.

Entitlement, Anger, and Personal Responsibility throughout the Life Cycle

In our twenties, we face the crisis of separating and individuating for the second time (the first separation-individuation is when we leave our infantile dependency and begin to form the core of our personality).[1] It is an emotionally challenging decade. For the young adult, identity consolidates into an adult self, an initial career path, and a committed love relationship. This is not uncommonly a turbulent and tortuous process, and therapy with the young adult involves providing a great deal of support and empathy while helping them identify what to bring along and what to leave behind from their mother and father (i.e., "What are the ways that I want to be like them, and what aspects of them should I reject as not being true to my identity?"), helping them to discover and define for themselves who they truly are.

The focus of therapy may include how to manage newfound freedom, facilitating a successful separation from the emotional and financial dependency on your parents, balancing inner desires with outer realities and responsibilities, and learning how to act authentically in love relationships.

Once the young adult (hopefully) grieves the parental relationships they longed for but didn't experience and begins to take responsibility for the direction and purpose of their life, there is newfound self-esteem that comes from the realization that they (not their parents) are now the masters of their destiny, laying out a course that will define their life. This is a liberating experience, immensely exciting yet frightening as they feel the pride that comes from supporting themselves and performing well at work.

Here are two examples of this principle in young adults.

Brenda's Story

Brenda was a twenty-five-year-old woman who entered therapy deeply depressed. She had been an exceptional student, excelling in high school and graduating magna cum laude from a prestigious university with a degree in business. She was a person of high moral character who suffered a series of setbacks in the "hookup culture," where she became appalled at how young men treated her and her friends. She became depressed over the difference between the world she imagined, characterized by honor, respect, and personal responsibility—the values she was raised with—and the social world she found in college, largely characterized by heartlessness, extreme selfishness, immediate sexual gratification, and disloyal behavior.

She fell in love with a young man in her sophomore year of college who had serious emotional problems and was later discovered to be using drugs. When Brenda learned that he had repeatedly cheated on her, she was emotionally devastated and blamed herself:

"I felt like I wasn't attractive enough," she said, "or exciting enough."

The confidence she had felt since high school evaporated, and she became significantly depressed but "toughed it out" until a year after graduation, when she entered therapy.

Brenda's depression was compounded by her difficulties in initially establishing a career path.

"Most of my friends are in medical or law school or investment banking," she explained. "I hated science and have no interest in law or finance. I feel like I deserve a prestigious career with a high salary, but I feel lost. My successful friends are just luckier than I am."

She waitressed at two upscale restaurants to support herself while applying for various sales positions, given her gift of gab and a belief that successful salespeople could make a lot of money.

First, Brenda tried out a sales position at a large insurance company that underchallenged her intellectually and felt like a creative

31

wasteland—which left her feeling despondent over her prospects in life. Her entry into corporate America was initially filled with idealism and hope that she would rapidly rise up the corporate ladder, but the realities of political infighting, jealous competitive rivalries, and the bureaucratic stifling of her creative sales ideas soon served to bring her down once again.

Brenda suffered an extreme narcissistic injury[2]—a blow to her self-esteem—in her transition from the top of her class to the bottom of the heap in the working world, and she began to blame her parents. She eventually withdrew from friends and family and began to gain weight.

"They worry too much—" (her father was a Holocaust survivor and was extremely overprotective) "—and are constantly giving advice that makes me feel worse and like they don't think I know how to make my own decisions. Like I'm completely incompetent. And they're right! They never let me date in high school or taught me what to expect, so I'm fumbling out on my own now. Sometimes, I think it would be easier to move to another city and start over, start fresh."

We began treatment with antidepressant medication and intensive psychotherapy, and I initially provided emotional support for her to develop an open, safe, and empathetic therapeutic relationship. We then transitioned to a deeper therapy, where Brenda began to explore the unconscious origins of her conflicts.

We learned that her entitlement was partly based in her belief that a high level of academic accomplishment would in and of itself deliver a powerful and prestigious professional position. Some of her entitlement also originated in how her parents would repeatedly tell her how wonderful she was and that she was destined for greatness. Brenda's competitive feelings—coming from a family of high achievers and being surrounded by friends who were pursuing careers in law, medicine, and finance—created additional emotional pressures.

Through our work together, she came to accept that her employers were not like her parents: "I realize now that a potential employer won't see me like my parents do. I have to prove my economic value."

In the course of therapy, she also began to learn how not to personalize insensitive treatment by others, instead recognizing that the sources of the cruel behavior originated in those people's emotional conflicts, not in her.

"Brenda," I explained, "some women are envious of your good looks, ambition, academic accomplishments, and immense innate talent. Others envy the fact that you come from a prominent family. Some of the young men you meet and fellow employees and managers try to manage their competitive envy by devaluing, constraining, and opposing you. Others objectify you sexually, never getting to know you as a person."

"I can see that now," she said. "It's hard for me not to take it personally, but I'm getting better at it. I understand, at least intellectually, that it's not about me; it's about them."

Over time, Brenda was able to give up her feelings of entitlement and to not feel so wounded when others treated her badly. She settled on a career path in marketing, obtained an entry-level position in a start-up that was entering a period of rapid growth, and she worked hard to impress those above her with her creativity and ingenuity. As of this writing, she is satisfied with her work life, has been growing more romantically involved with a seemingly solid young man, and is considering applying to MBA programs with a focus on marketing.

* * *

Through our work in talk therapy, Brenda was able to develop greater emotional maturity and to recover from the inevitable narcissistic injuries of young adulthood. The story of Peter further illustrates some of the principles of psychotherapy with this age group.

Peter's Story

Peter was in his early twenties, and had a number of longstanding emotional and physical challenges, when he first came to see me. He had been born with cerebral palsy and needed arm braces to walk. Beginning in his childhood, unfeeling students frequently made fun of him at school. As a result of severe ADHD and learning disabilities, Peter had serious difficulty passing his college classes, and he became extremely depressed when he flunked out.

As an adult child living at home, he was excessively emotionally and financially dependent on his overprotective mother. And to further challenge his self-esteem, his brother was a surgeon, and his twin sister was a successful businesswoman, both having graduated from top universities. Peter was also wrestling with the emotional implications of a major life decision—whether he should apply for and accept the government-funded disability payments that he was entitled to receive or become self-sufficient through his own initiative.

We began to work together in psychotherapy to help Peter separate from his mother and figure out an identity that was right for him. We also treated his ADHD with stimulant medication.

"I need to become my own man," was how he put his desire for the pride that comes with independence. "Depending on disability payments would make me feel like I can't support myself. I don't know if I could look at myself in the mirror if I let the government pay my way. Is that any better than my mom doing it? I need to do it on my own."

In the course of his psychotherapy, Peter grieved never having a "normal" childhood. "The constant mocking when I was in school still makes me feel sad but also angry at the kids who did it. I also feel like my brother and sister are good at everything they do, and it seems to come so easily to them, while I'm stuck at home, struggling to get by."

Peter worked through these traumas and jealousies and gained independence. He secured an administrative position at a financial services firm and moved out of his parents' house, which filled him with enormous pride.

Through psychotherapy, patients like Peter may confront the emotional impact of their disabilities and develop the strengths necessary to gain greater independence. In the process, some may benefit by turning down government entitlements and services that may make them feel like a chronic invalid. Although such assistance originated in compassion, it sometimes perpetuates dependencies that preclude the pride that comes from self-sufficiency.

* * *

In our forties and fifties, we face midlife, where there may be an existential crisis characterized by questions like "Is this all there is to my life?" We may feel that we have not achieved all we deserve to achieve and may blame it on others. We may experience a lack of meaning and purpose, feel empty inside, and not feel as "alive" as we did in our twenties and thirties.

Therapy may involve coming to terms with unconscious feelings of anger and entitlement and uncovering passions that can be lived out through a job change or finding a new career, discovering a new hobby, or rekindling earlier passions that were subordinated to the demands of establishing your career and raising a family. One can also find the courage to leave behind an oppressive and depleting love relationship, to begin to live out a newfound sense of freedom. Following is an example of a middle-aged patient that illustrates these points.

Michael's Story

Michael was forty-five years old when he entered therapy, suffering from depression and anxiety. When he was a child, his parents divorced.

"I never saw my dad much after that," he said. "My mother took on a series of live-in boyfriends, and they never cared much for my sister and me. I never felt like I belonged at home after the divorce. Yeah, I know—typical sob story, but that's why I'm here."

Michael's early life was joyless, except for his remarkable athletic abilities, which brought him the admiration and camaraderie of coaches and teammates. He attended college, majoring in computer science, and partied excessively, which resulted in missed classes and poor grades. He barely graduated—in part, because of low self-esteem and the unconscious belief that he was not worthy of success. These feelings had developed in childhood as a result of his father's abandonment and the frequent criticism and abuse from his mother's boyfriends. Following college, he began to distinguish himself in the world of high technology, married a coworker, and fathered three children.

"I'm terrific at my job, but I can't seem to get my bosses to realize that," he said, describing his struggles with authority figures at work. "I explain to them how the job should be done, and they just won't listen. Maybe I come across as angry, but I'm always right. I can't believe several of them fired me over that; I was just trying to improve those places."

Although he loved being a father and husband and was successful in these areas of his life, Michael's professional life was marred by a series of setbacks that left him depressed and suffering from a multitude of physical symptoms.

Finally, he settled into a position. "It's a large government contractor, and this kind of place seems to be really stable. They've got a bunch of long-term contracts and employ thousands of IT professionals, so it should be a slam dunk. I just know that I'll become incredibly important to them."

Paradoxically, he became even more depressed in this position. The enormous indifference of the federal bureaucracy and the outright opposition to and criticism of his initiatives by government employees served to unconsciously remind him of his father's indifference and the criticism and devaluation from his mother's boyfriends.

"I want to show them what I can do—like I did on the playing field—but the bureaucracy keeps getting in the way. I'm just a number here. There's a major contract, and I've got some great ideas for it, but they're not interested in anything I have to offer."

Through difficult and painful work in psychotherapy, Michael was able to grieve the parents he longed for but never had. His sessions were filled with sadness and anger as he worked through these feelings and expressed his deep longing to be liberated from the bonds of his childhood relationships. As he worked through his angry feelings, he was able to cast aside his feelings of entitlement. He began to take responsibility for his actions, recognized how he sabotaged one former position after another and how he unconsciously selected uncaring and authoritarian company cultures that replicated the dynamics of his family of origin. After three years of intensive work, he felt more confident and free to explore his passions.

"I feel like I own my life now," he said. "I've just started as the chief information officer of a small family-owned company. They treat everyone like family—a *healthy* family."

Michael's new employer operated in a niche that was being buffeted by rapidly changing marketplace dynamics, and he quickly assumed a position of power and respect as he began to guide them to meet the future. No longer unconsciously positioning himself in the workforce as an entitled young boy, perpetually grief stricken and angry over being abandoned and criticized and railing against authority figures, he had taken control of his life and was now the authority figure himself.

Through psychotherapy, Michael was able to change his professional identity and leave behind authoritarian cultures to join a small firm that valued each individual's contribution and where he felt a sense of an unlimited promise. He had learned what constituted his authentic self and was now living it out.

A powerful unconscious that controls your actions and choices is an internal shackle that may impair your personal freedom. This is all the more true when you have unconscious feelings of entitlement.

Begin to Heal

What relevance does this have for you? Use your workbook to journal your thoughts and address these prompts and questions, which will help you explore the effects of entitlement and anger in your own life.

Step 1: Think about your own entitlement.

If you believe that you may have entitlement issues of your own, begin to think about how this has affected specific relationships at work and with loved ones. Think back to relationships that went badly, and put the relationship under the microscope to see what you may have contributed to the negative outcome. Exactly what happened? What are the details?

Step 2: Look for patterns.

Is there a pattern to your relationships at work or in love? Do they develop in a particular way and then blow up? Describe the pattern.

Step 3: How do you feel?

Do you frequently feel undervalued, cheated, or taken advantage of? Describe the relationships this occurs in and what happens. Is there a pattern? How do you behave as a result of these feelings?

Step 4: Recognize and own your feelings of anger.

Do you harbor feelings of envy and bitterness toward those you perceive as more successful? If so, how does this affect your feelings about yourself and your prospects in life? How are these feelings expressed at work and at home? Do they affect your behavior? If so, how?

Step 5: Address feelings of entitlement.

Do you feel that the cards are stacked against you in life or that what happens to you is unfair and unwarranted? When did these feelings begin? Can you determine their origin? If so, describe what was happening in your life at that time. Did one or both of your parents feel this way? If so, how would they manifest these feelings? Please describe in detail.

Step 6: Take control of your life.

If you answered yes to one or more of the above questions, it may be that feelings of anger and entitlement are undermining your ability to grow and develop at work or in love. If this is the case, the first and most important step you can take is to realize that you are in charge of your life and responsible for its course. Are you willing to take this step? Write out how you might begin to do so. If you are unwilling, what is getting in the way?

Step 7: Embrace empathy.

Your behaviors are influenced in part by how you view the motives of others. It is essential that you view each and every other person in your life as someone who has their own hopes, dreams, fears, goals, and emotional conflicts. Not every situation or interaction is about you; it is also about them. Begin to learn about what others in your life need and value, and begin to provide it, thereby making yourself more valuable to them. Can you commit to taking this important step? Write down the names of the most important people in your life, and then list under each name what you believe they most need and value and what you can do to help meet those needs.[3]

Step 8: Create balanced relationships.

Once you have completed step 7, focus on creating win–win relationships, where others' needs are considered, as opposed to just thinking about what you can get or what you are being denied. Are you willing to create win–win relationships at work and at home? List five important people at work and at home, and under each name, write out how you might begin to engage them in a win–win conversation. What would constitute a win for them? For you?

Step 9: Take responsibility.

If you make a mistake, own it, take full responsibility, and indicate in a serious way that you intend to do better next time. Saying "I'm sorry" can be monumental and even life altering—particularly if you rarely utter those words. It can begin to ease chronic tension in relationships at home and at work but will only be effective if you also begin to change your behavior. List events that upset you, where you blame someone else for what happened, and then next to each event, write out how you share in the responsibility for the outcome.

Step 10: Hold yourself to high standards.

Dress and behave in a professional manner at work, and hold yourself to a high standard when relating to colleagues, focusing more on listening to them and working to understand their perspectives and needs than on getting your needs met. List at least five ways you can commit to acting more professionally at work, starting tomorrow.

Step 11: Improve yourself.

Develop new skills that will increase your value at your current job or with future employers. A supervisor of mine once said, "It is better to be in demand than demanding." List three skills that would make you more valuable and marketable, and commit to when you will begin to acquire them.

Step 12: Learn about your behavior from others.

Wrestle with the answers to these questions, and if appropriate, seek candid feedback from friends and loved ones. List five questions that you would like them to answer that will provide valuable feedback to you in learning more about whether you come across as angry and entitled, and ask them to provide examples and details.

If, despite your best efforts, your anger and entitlement continue to sabotage your happiness, seek professional help. You might need more guidance to find the solution that works for you, and your therapist can provide that.

Preventing and Treating Entitlement in Our Children

As parents, we have the awesome responsibility of shaping our children's personalities and imparting to them a value system that they will take into the world to serve them for life. During their childhood and adolescence, the values that we desire them to adopt may be in direct conflict with those they witness on television, in school, online, and through the many other influences that bombard them on a daily basis.

We would like our children to develop emotional maturity, treat others fairly and with kindness, have a strong work ethic, become independent thinkers, use good judgment, become capable of mature love for a significant other, earn their way through life, be loyal to their friends and loved ones, develop and maintain deep friendships, and lead a life where they will act honorably and achieve self-respect and the respect of others. We want them to understand the value of hard work, grit,[4] and a determined effort that is sustained over time. We would like to prevent them from becoming entitled or developing other attributes of a narcissistic personality.

If you would like your children to grow up to lead virtuous lives, it is vital that you act virtuously. Because life can be painful and difficult, acting honorably can be quite challenging at times, and we parents are tested in many ways and inevitably fail from time to time. We may be called on to stand diametrically opposed to the values our children are exposed to elsewhere. It takes courage to take a stand with your child against many of these values that conflict with your own. It requires a willingness on your part to institute and enforce rules that will be unpopular, will be different from the rules set by many of their friends' parents, and will provoke pushback—particularly when they are teenagers.

There may be times when you feel that you have little or no influence over your child's life, compared with all of these other forces. And at any given time, you are only as happy as your least happy child. Yet even with the ups and downs we experience in our relationships with our children over the course of a lifetime, we can continue to be a strong positive influence. It is important that you live out the value system you want to impart to your children and set an example for them in your day-to-day interactions with them and with your spouse. In other words, you need to *walk the talk.*

Raising a Responsible Child

If you are a parent with young children, you would like to impart to them a value system that will carry them well throughout their lives and ultimately enable them to develop emotionally mature adult relationships. A wonderful method is to share nightly reading sessions with your children. Try reading from William J. Bennett's *The Book of Virtues.* Bennett addresses how values such as responsibility, courage, compassion, honesty, friendship, persistence, and faith are essential traits of good character. The book offers children examples of good and bad, right and wrong, through hundreds of stories that come from many sources—from the Bible to American history, from Greek mythology to English poetry, from fairy tales to modern fiction.

If your children are too young to read, begin by reading them some of the chapter headings and story titles to get them excited about what stories they would like you to read aloud. Encourage them to take turns choosing each successive evening. If they are old enough to read aloud, have them take turns selecting and reading stories that resonate with them. Make this a nightly tradition in your household; it will impart a reliable and memorable set of moral reference points that will help anchor them in the ideals you value.

If your child is an adolescent, imparting values can be more challenging. Many teens behave narcissistically. Some of this behavior may be age appropriate, because teens are struggling to convince themselves that they are not dependent on adults. This typically manifests itself with rule breaking, openly or secretly challenging your authority, angry entitled outbursts, demanding to be given certain freedoms or material items, refusing to do chores around the house, and asking for privileges enjoyed by their friends that you feel are excessive or unwarranted.

Begin to Heal

Here are some steps that you can try to encourage them to take responsibility for their lives. Take out your journal to write out your ideas and answers. If you are married, be certain to discuss your answers and proposed solutions with your spouse prior to implementing them.

Step 1: Listen.

Begin by patiently listening to their troubles, angry feelings, and grievances, and try not to be provoked into getting angry and dismissive. (This is really hard. Teens can be so provocative at times, can't they?!) When was the last time you were provoked into anger by your child? Describe the details. How might you have handled it differently by trying to empathize and understand?

Step 2: Give support.

Be willing to support their self-assertion and their feelings as long as they are not disrespectful toward you, and tell them you are proud of their willingness to put their thoughts and feelings into words rather than acting on them. Think of a recent argument. How might you have encouraged them to express their angry feelings in a respectful way that would help you listen to them vent and not lose your cool?

Step 3: Pick your battles.

Stand for values that you believe strongly in, and be willing to be flexible and let go of issues that are not as important. Which rules do you feel are inviolable and why are they important to you? What is the principle behind each of them? Which rules are less vital, where you are willing to be more flexible and negotiate their terms?

Step 4: Be honest.

Be willing to be open and honest about why you believe that the rules you have established are necessary. You have established them out of love, caring, and protectiveness and will loosen certain rules as they get older and demonstrate their ability to behave responsibly. Be willing to discuss modifications to the rules, and if their proposed modifications make sense, be willing to agree. Develop a specific plan for one or more of the rules, whereby you trade increasing freedom for your teen in return for their demonstrating increased responsibility. List the steps in the plan, and then discuss them with your teen.

Step 5: Reward, don't just punish.

Rewards work better than punishments in bringing about desired behavior.[5] Reward behaviors that you would like to see more of, and punish behaviors that break the rules. The degree of punishment should be commensurate with the magnitude of the rule breaking—proportional to the "crime." Try to remember what it was like when you were a teenager as you evaluate the fairness of a punishment. Develop a system of rewards and punishments for specific behaviors, and sit down and discuss it with your teen to hear their thoughts and feelings, then begin to implement them. Be consistent.[6]

Step 6: Communicate.

Encourage your teen to think about themselves and their life and the impact of their behavior on others. Get into a habit of regular discussions—maybe after school over a snack or in the car on the way to a sports practice—where you inquire about how their life is going, empathize with any struggles they are having, and help them connect the dots between cause and effect in their life in a noncritical way. Keep these conversations relaxed and informal; if it feels like an inquisition, they'll shut down.

Step 7: Accept disagreement.

Don't be afraid to have your child get angry and even hateful toward you at times in response to your standing firm in enforcing rules. This can be really tough for any parent to bear, and it may feel easier at times just to give in, but it is not your job to be their friend. Unconsciously, they are grateful that you are in control and in charge at a time in their life when they feel so out of control and confused.

What are five steps that you could take to calm down when you're under attack? How can you take the conversation less personally and put it into the context of their life struggles? List some of the causes of their angry feelings that have nothing to do with you.

Step 8: Further incentivize good behavior.

As they gradually give up entitled behavior and act responsibly, find additional ways to reward them. The idea is to incentivize adult-like behavior wherever possible with praise and expressions of pride. In this way, they will take increasing responsibility for their life, which, of course, is the foundation of their becoming an independent adult. Make a concerted effort over the next week to praise good behaviors on their part, and write down how they respond. How might you remind yourself to continue praising good behavior beyond the end of the week?

I hope that this session has been helpful to you in understanding the destructive effects of anger and entitlement. Hopefully, the tools I provided will assist you in charting a new and more rewarding course.

You are beginning to understand the role of childhood traumatic experiences in shaping one's experience of themselves and the world. Some of the stories that follow will further illustrate how these experiences are addressed in treatment and how we can learn to overcome them.

SESSION FOUR

Help Your Child Following an Emotionally Disturbing Experience

One of the most influential psychoanalysts of the twentieth century, Erik Erikson, described the unfolding development of a human being in eight stages across the life cycle. Erikson described the interplay between individual emotional development and social experience to bring about new skills in each stage and how the proper or improper development in prior stages can affect our development in later stages. Failure to resolve the conflicts of a prior stage may resurface to worsen an emotional crisis in a later stage[1] (we will discuss that failure more in sessions 10 and 11). In this session, I will help you become a more effective parent when your child experiences an emotionally distressing event, so that the risk of the emotional crisis being carried forward to disrupt later stages in their life is reduced.

It is important for parents to create a protective envelope or shield around younger children in their most formative years, to bring them an increased feeling of stability and security,[2] particularly in the face of emotionally disturbing experiences such as bullying, betrayal, being cruelly ostracized, and the death of a pet or family member. How does a parent best respond to these upsets, and when is a psychiatric evaluation warranted?

First and most important, provide your child with a supportive and empathetic response to their emotional pain following such a trauma. Be a good and active listener. Don't be afraid to share your own feelings about the loss, but be careful not to burden your child if you are having difficulty coping. Most often, this approach, along with the support of friends, other family members, and teachers, will enable your child to get through the traumatic event without the need for therapy and will help them become more resilient.

Is there a way to predict which children are at risk for developing posttraumatic stress disorder (PTSD)? A parental history of trauma-related stress is a risk factor for the development and persistence of PTSD in children and adolescents who have undergone a traumatic event,[3] as a parent's capacity to create a feeling of emotional safety and security in their child and to emotionally empathize with the child's fear and anxiety may be diminished.

Although some children and teenagers spontaneously recover from PTSD over time, the results suggest that victims with a parental history of anxiety disorders, including generalized anxiety disorder, obsessive-compulsive disorder, PTSD of their own, and phobias, may deserve special attention from mental-health professionals, since they may be at heightened risk for developing PTSD after traumatic experiences.

If you have a history of an anxiety disorder, you may also want to consider a psychiatric evaluation and treatment for yourself following the traumatic event, to prevent developing PTSD yourself and to ensure that you can maintain effective parenting.

Beth's Story

Here is a story about a child who suffered through an emotionally disturbing experience and how, together, we helped her recover. Beth had just turned thirteen when she first arrived for therapy after being dragged into my office by her mother and father about a week after the start of the school year. She was refusing to go back to school due to a traumatic event she had first experienced at age ten and that had recently happened again. During much of the first session, this shy eighth grader either looked down at the floor or glared at me. Teenage patients have countless ways of testing the patience and resolve of their therapists (and, of course, their parents), and Beth was no exception.

Taking a deep breath, I began. "Beth, coming to see me is really hard, and this is probably the last place on Earth you want to be— sitting here with some strange doctor—and feeling put under a spotlight even more than you already have been at school. Your mom called me the other day, worried about what was happening to you at school and what you are feeling inside, and I am here to try to understand what has been done to you to make you feel so bad and to try to help you feel better. Would you mind telling me a little bit about what happened? I promise not to judge you in any way. If I am not doing a good job at understanding you, please feel free to set me straight."

And with that, Beth began to talk. Once she began, she didn't want to stop.

"Three years ago, when I was in the fifth grade, one of the other kids in my class started passing around a note about me. I was minding my own business; I didn't do anything to deserve this."

"What did the note say?" I asked.

"It said that . . . in the field behind the school building . . . that I had touched Joey Wilton's penis. In class everyone began laughing and looking at me. I grabbed the note, read it, and said it was a lie;

I never did such a thing. Then one of the boys in the class, who's always acting like a jerk, said that I had once asked him if I could touch his penis and that he had turned me down."

This was another complete lie but elicited even more laughter, and it was a crushing humiliation for Beth. As she told me this story, she burst into tears. Her mother tried to comfort her, and in my own mind, I recalled a time when I was bullied in the schoolyard and some tough kids trapped me in a jungle gym. They wouldn't let me out to go home and kept laughing. I remembered how sad and helpless and angry I had felt.

"Beth," I told her, "How horrible that must have been for you! Those boys were so cruel. It feels terribly humiliating to be laughed at by your peers, and you probably just wanted to disappear. It is so sad and infuriating. I am sorry that they did that to you and appreciate your telling me about it."

Her teacher had scolded the class as a whole but never reported the boy who created the original note or the one who had made the lewd comments.

"She didn't say anything to help me," Beth said. "And neither of the boys in class got in trouble for what they did. She just pretended like it didn't happen and left me to deal with everyone laughing at me in the hallway."

I empathized with Beth by saying, "How upsetting it must be that your teacher, an adult who you count on to protect you, didn't take action against those boys. She was wrong in not defending you, and it is very unfair that the boys got away with it."

"That's how adults are. At least I know now not to trust people. But I started having bad dreams right after. I couldn't go to school for about a week; I'd panic on the way to class." In the second week, she would sit in her mother's car outside the entrance to the school for many minutes ("It felt like an eternity") before finally entering.

"For the rest of the year, many of my so-called friends shunned me, but I kept going to class anyway.

"The next year, it all seemed to blow over, and I had two years without any drama. I made some new friends, and middle school was just the typical sucky place that I guess it is for everybody."

Then, Beth began to tell me about what happened recently, and my heart sank.

"Eighth grade, unfortunately, was a different story. When I went to math, the two boys from the fifth grade—the note passer and the liar—were not only sitting in the room next to each other, but they started whispering to the kids around them, nodding at me, and all of them began laughing again. All I could make out was, 'Yes, that's her; she's the one.'"

Beth felt devastated and immediately went up to the teacher's desk.

"I told her that I needed to see the nurse because my stomach hurt. I began crying and ran out of the classroom and had the nurse call my mother to pick me up and take me home. I couldn't stand how bad those kids made me feel."

The ugly experience and feelings that Beth thought she had left behind three years earlier came crashing back in on her. She then refused to go to school, which is why her mother brought her in to see me.

"Beth, I am so sorry that this happened to you yet again after those couple of years when you felt that it was all behind you. It is hard to imagine how sad and angry this must make you feel and how horrifying it must be to relive all over again what happened a few years ago, when you believed that incident would never come up again. The level of cruelty of those boys is despicable. They should be ashamed of themselves and should be punished for what they've done." I then asked her if it was okay if her mother left the room so that we could talk alone. She agreed, and when her mother left, Beth initially said nothing and continued to look at the floor.

> ♪ **Session Soundtrack** ♪
>
> The song "Skyscraper," sung by Demi Lovato, an ardent antibullying campaigner, is a heartfelt and poignant depiction of how a young person feels when faced with heartbreaking sadness and pain caused by someone who is trying to tear them down or break them. The lyrics relate to a girl who is "broken" and "bleeding," who feels there is nothing left for her but is determined to rise up toward the clouds once again.
>
> Visitv DrBruceKehr.com/music-3 for audio files
> and further discussion of the soundtracks.

I sometimes share songs with my patients in treatment, as I've shared with you in the "Session Soundtracks" (see the box above). I played Demi Lovato's "Skyscraper" for her, and at one point during the song, Beth looked up at me with such sadness in her eyes that it broke my heart. I felt like crying too and wished that I could just hold her and comfort her. (This was a **countertransference reaction** inside of me that I used to feel more compassion for her; to act on these feelings would have been countertherapeutic.) When the song was over, I again told her how sorry I was that this had happened to her at all, noting that some deeply humiliating events had once happened to me when I was her age when some boys bullied me at the bus stop (I didn't go into any details) and that I understood exactly how she felt.

Beth then began opening up to me (whereby she would free associate, talking about whatever came into her mind), weeping over her plight, feeling hopeless about ever going back to school, wanting to be homeschooled, and feeling furious at her parents. She recalled how unempathic her father had been when he first learned of the traumatic event that took place in the fifth grade.

"At the dinner table, he was angry and told me not to be so sensitive and to toughen up and get back to school the next day."

She ran out of the dining room in tears and locked herself in her bedroom. Her mother then yelled at her father for his lack of sensitivity, which only made Beth feel worse, and in the weeks that followed, her mother punished her father by actively challenging his authority in front of the children.

Beth then felt at an all-time low. As she recounted these events, openly crying and feeling angry at her parents, I encouraged her to express to me how she felt toward her classmates as well. She then willingly vented her fury: "I wish I had kicked and punched those two dickheads! They had no right to say those things about me. And the teacher should have done something. That's her job, isn't it—to protect us?"

Here was yet another adult who had let her down! I empathized with these feelings and told her that, when I had been bullied at her age, my father had suggested that I take a martial arts course and began to teach me how to box, to toughen me up and build my confidence, and it had really helped me to stand up to those boys at the bus stop.

"How would you feel about trying a martial arts class like that?" I asked. She liked the idea, and we agreed that I would bring it up with her parents at the next family session.

Beth and I began to develop a kind of friendship in our sessions—the kind that can really help an adolescent feel more comfortable. Sharing music helped immensely in establishing our bond. As Beth became more open, animated, and courageous, she was able to confront her parents with her feelings in conjoint family sessions. Although I was worried about whether they could tolerate her disappointment and anger and work through it or would, instead, prematurely yank her out of therapy, I began to feel hopeful for Beth's recovery.

We also explored the origins of bullying behavior—the emotional and psychological factors that drove some kids to bully others—and what she knew about the two perpetrators who had humiliated her in front of her classmates. What emerged was that the two boys came from broken homes, where it was rumored that they had been repeatedly beaten by their fathers. She recalled that these boys had preyed on other sensitive kids as well and seemed to single out those who were really good students—the more intelligent, sensitive, and thoughtful kids—kids just like her. In contrast, the boys were consistently at the bottom of the class.

"I think they try to make themselves feel good at the expense of others," she said.

And in response, I said, "Beth, that's a really good observation! Their self-esteem must be fragile. They probably have little self-respect because of their family backgrounds—being bullied and abused by their fathers—and because they do so poorly in school."

She took some comfort and even a bit of satisfaction from these realizations. Much later, she was even able to develop some compassion toward the boys.

Because Beth was suffering from severe insomnia with panic attacks at night and throughout the day, along with symptoms of depression and some suicidal thoughts, I prescribed clonazepam (to treat the panic attacks) and paroxetine (to treat the depression and school phobia), and we agreed to meet for weekly therapy. We arranged for her to temporarily be homeschooled through the Home and Hospital Program in the county schools, and I began to teach her how to breathe deeply and use autorelaxation techniques when she felt anxious or panicky.[4]

I convinced Beth's parents to enroll her in a martial arts program, which I believed would help boost her self-esteem and restore some self-respect. Once she was enrolled, she began to feel better. We initiated what is called **exposure and response prevention therapy**[5] experiences: We would have her ride with her mother to the front of the school, imagine that she was going inside, and as she would begin to feel panicky, she would take slow, deep breaths and use the relaxation exercises to calm down. Once she felt calm, her mother would drive them home.

In addition, I supported her trying out for the girl's hockey team. She was very fast, had great eye–hand coordination, and could explore yet another outlet for her anger, as well as develop another source of pride (which certainly couldn't hurt).

The combination of the medication to block the panic attacks, the insight-oriented psychotherapy to help her understand the underlying motives of the other children, and the exposure therapy all helped Beth to begin to attend school again. She still hated middle school (does any child like it?) but was able to avoid engaging with the two boys and dismissed any of their hateful comments as resulting from their sad and abusive home situations. Thanks to the hockey and the karate lessons, Beth began to present a "Don't mess with me" attitude, carrying herself with more pride and determination.

Begin to Heal

Perhaps you have a child like Beth or are concerned that your child may be developing a school phobia or that they are coping badly with bullying or other stressors. You may feel distraught and helpless, unsure about how to proceed. What should you do? Use your workbook to write down your thoughts and responses to these prompts and questions, as you take the following steps:

Step 1: You can *feel* angry, but don't *act* angry.

Try not to get angry at your child because of your own feelings of helplessness or frustration over how they react to a traumatic experience. A pattern can develop where you repeatedly get angry when you may be upset over what has happened to them or feel stressed for other reasons. They will interpret this anger as directed at them. Are you unconsciously acting toward them in a way that you were treated by your mother or father? If so, how?

Step 2: Put yourself in their shoes.

Enter their world in a caring, empathetic, and supportive fashion. What hurdles did you face when you were their age? Were there any traumatic experiences? How did you cope with them? How might it be different for your child in today's world, with the heightened complexity of computer technology and social media? After you've considered this, encourage your child to openly discuss their feelings. Writing out their feelings or drawing a picture if they like to draw or are younger can be a helpful preliminary step toward open sharing.

Step 3: Find someone for them to talk to.

If your child is resistant to sharing their thoughts and feelings with you, would they be more likely to open up with your spouse, a neighbor or family friend, or a coach? The love of a grandparent for a grandchild is perhaps the purest love of all. It can be lifesaving, particularly in a seriously depressed and suicidal child, adolescent, or young adult who has turned away from one or both parents. Is there a grandparent who might be able to reach your child? Try to pick someone your child has a great deal of trust in and who they may feel less conflicted and emotionally safe with.

Step 4: Find a way to connect.

If your child rejects both of those approaches, another option is to share a special piece of music with them where the lyrics speak to their life situation and emotional state. This will help your child feel less alone and self-conscious. With Beth, our listening to music really opened the door into her heart. Sharing music with your child may also convey your active empathy and willingness to enter their world to understand. List some artists and songs that could reach them, and if you are unsure which artists appeal to them, ask one of their siblings or friends for guidance. Alternately, you could take your child to one of their favorite activities, then casually ask how life's treating them. In the past, where might you have taken them where they opened up to you?

Step 5: Support; don't suffocate.

Some parents have an overprotective parenting style. In order to build your child's self-esteem, give empathy and emotional support while encouraging them to take on new challenges and figure out their own solutions. Help them over hurdles they can't overcome themselves while being careful not to rush in and rescue them from situations they can manage on their own. Where do you provide too much guidance and support? In what areas might your child build more confidence if you back off? Conversely, are there areas where they are floundering and could benefit from more of your assistance? If so, how might you provide this?

Step 6: Encourage persistence.

Challenge your child to persist in the face of adversity and provide support when the going gets tough, without being judgmental if they complain about how hard it is. How might you be more encouraging instead? List some specific ideas. What might you say to let them know that you are proud of their efforts to hang in there?

Step 7: Seek professional help.

If none of these techniques work, and your child has one or more of the following signs or symptoms—anxiety attacks, social withdrawal, trouble sleeping, refusing to attend school, difficulty concentrating, frequent anger outbursts, declining school performance—then it is time to obtain professional help. Your child may resist this step, already feeling painfully self-conscious or singled out and may really dig in their heels and refuse to go. It is important that you and your spouse agree that this step is nonnegotiable, and then offer to go in with your son or daughter, saying that it is help for the family, which will also include other siblings in the sessions. Insisting that the entire family enter therapy will help your child overcome feelings of shame or blame. Even with everyone present, the therapist will have an opportunity to bond with your child and, over time, will work to win them over into accepting individual therapy. Once they've entered individual therapy, don't be surprised if they rarely admit to you that they find the sessions helpful. This is a common attempt to save face. Their regular attendance is a good indication that you've made the right choice in therapist.

It makes no sense to treat a child individually and send them back into the home environment without parental involvement in the therapeutic process. You need guidance to better parent your troubled child and to help them heal their emotional wounds. You need a place where you can learn, get emotional support, and grow yourself. This joint commitment will also enable you and your spouse to coordinate your approaches to your child and to support one another rather than openly engage in conflict, which can just worsen matters for all concerned.

If all of you stick with it, better times lie around the corner. It can also help to talk with trusted friends to get support and share ideas about how to more effectively parent. You will never be perfect, and we all make mistakes as parents. The goal is to keep learning and improving and not have to feel alone with the awesome responsibility of raising a child.

I hope that today's session was helpful. When we meet next time, I will explore with you how a mood disorder such as depression develops; what that feels like inside; how its origins relate to biological, childhood, and environmental events; and how to help you and your child develop healthier self-esteem. I look forward to seeing you again.

SESSION FIVE

Heal an Existential Crisis in a Young Adult

A number of highly talented young adults are living through what might be characterized as an **existential crisis**,[1] feeling that they can no longer go on with life as they have been—that maybe they've been living a lie. They feel that their identity—the way they've come to know themselves—is shattered, and they don't have a new one to replace it. They may find themselves in a suicidal crisis and feel that the "star quality" that once made them and their parents feel so proud is gone or nothing more than an unbearable burden. The hopes and aspirations that they shared with their parents—the ones that had been praised or lauded—have seemingly been abandoned, and the values that had once driven them toward excellence are nowhere to be found. They may withdraw from their friends, barely attending high school or college classes and wanting to stay in bed. They may also feel enraged at their parents and at life itself and scared that they have no one to turn to. Their life as they and their loved ones have come to know it grinds to a halt, and they don't see any way out.

> ♪ **Session Soundtrack** ♪
>
> The song "Demons," by Imagine Dragons, poignantly depicts what these young people are feeling inside as they are filled with the depression and disillusionment that come with an existential crisis. The lyrics of this song capture their transformation from highly accomplished "saints of gold" to depressed, angry, and disillusioned "cards (that) all fold," as what was once certain has now vanished. They may feel that their dreams have failed to materialize and that they lack the energy or will to pursue new ones. Lives previously filled with excitement and accomplishment appear to inexplicably crash and burn; these young people suddenly seem like hollowed out versions of their former selves.
>
> Visit DrBruceKehr.com/music-4 for audio files
> and further discussion of the soundtracks.

If you are the mother or father, grandparent, or aunt or uncle of one of these young adults, what you are observing likely feels frightening, confusing, sad, and inexplicable. It is a time of high anxiety and great uncertainty for everyone involved. You may feel that you are about to lose or have already lost your child and will never get them back again. In this chapter, you will come to better understand how therapy can help those suffering from an existential crisis and what you can do to help as well.

Identifying Those Who Suffer

Those who suffer from this condition are typically high-achieving young men and women in their mid- to late teens or early twenties, with perfectionist tendencies and impressive track records of academic and extracurricular success. Typically, these young people have been highly praised by adults and driven to excel to please their parents and teachers, never having thought much about what would make them happy. Their years of compliant behavior may have exacted a kind of psychic toll; they harbored anger or rage deep inside that was never openly expressed for fear of loss of love from adults or of the prestige that comes from high levels of accomplishment. They hide their feelings from their parents and even from themselves; living with adulation is gratifying, and they don't want to give that up. Eventually, the "beast" or "demon" inside finally begins to emerge in the form of depression, anger, alcohol or drug use, or sudden and seemingly inexplicable oppositional behavior.

Some of these young adults reveal a long history of having concealed an intense anxiety over a failure to perform at the very highest level. At times, this anxiety escalates into panic attacks—particularly when they fail to turn in a top performance, which subsequently causes them to become severely self-critical and filled with self-loathing. After years of near-flawless performances, they became their own "tough act to follow." They lived in constant fear of being given a poor grade—for some, even a B is considered a failure—and were filled with dread over losing their "star" status.

Other fears include disappointing their parents and whether they would continue to be loved (or would be severely criticized) if they let up on their perfectionistic strivings. These youths often display one or more of the following traits: emotional sensitivity, delayed social maturity in dating, feeling unpopular, being identified as "nerds" or "kiss ups," favoring adults over peers, and possessing an unusual degree of empathy and compassion. At times, there may be a history of attention deficit disorder, inattentive type, which is masked by high intelligence and a strong work ethic.

These youths "hit a wall" at one of their lives' important transition points—graduating high school, as a freshman or sophomore in college, or entering into the "real world" following college graduation. Seemingly without warning, they become depressed, angry, and lost. The existential crisis may be precipitated by extreme disappointment in one or more love relationships; the death of a loved one, such as a friend, parent, or grandparent; a serious setback during the transition from high school to college, college to graduate school, or school to the job market. At times, there may be no apparent precipitant. Commonly, in one form or another, there is a loss of an ideal, and what previously provided meaning, guidance, and purpose no longer works and is actively repudiated. They may be tormented by the question, "What will I do with my life now?"

How Therapy Can Help

If a young person feels suicidal or is failing to function at school, a psychiatric evaluation and talk therapy should be initiated as soon as possible. Treatment typically involves prescription medication and psychotherapy focused on establishing an open and nonjudgmental rapport. This connection can help the young adult comprehend what has happened to them and assist them in making sense of the dramatic turn of events in their relationship with themselves and the world around them.

As was mentioned in previous sessions, listening to music that portrays a patient's inner emotional struggles can be a way to accelerate the development of trust. The music creates a friendly and nonthreatening atmosphere that encourages the open expression of feelings, often initiated through the exploration of a song's lyrics.

The early phase of treatment may also include initiating the judicious use of antidepressant, antianxiety, antipsychotic, or mood-stabilizing medication to help with overwhelming symptoms of anxiety and depression or mood instability. As the therapy unfolds, the young adult begins to differentiate between values that they were taught and values that they feel truly represent their core personality.

Slowly but surely, they begin to identify their own sources of happiness, as opposed to just trying to please their teachers and parents. Through empathetic listening and compassionate acceptance of their disillusionment and anger by the therapist, they begin to distinguish between former passions that actually belong with their parents and newfound passions that are theirs alone. They leave behind their False Self and embrace their True Self.[2] Rejecting the more traditional paths into self-sufficient adulthood, they experiment and explore; they wander. They make mistakes, which is part of the process of learning about who they really are.

The young adult newly discovers meaning, purpose, satisfaction, and happiness through self-knowledge and a greater understanding of their place in the world. These overly perfectionistic young adults learn how to play and to love aspects of themselves unrelated to performance and stardom. Their journey will be filled with potholes and unexpected twists and turns. But with patient and persistent hard work, they eventually cast aside their demons and relaunch themselves—this time with an aim that is true.

Parents must learn to tolerate and accept ambiguity and uncertainty, feelings of great helplessness, and to recognize that they have no control over their child's life. You must let go while continuing to provide love and support. There may be many sleepless nights as these young adults get in touch with their repressed rage and begin to express the "demons" that are lurking in a dark place inside of them. Along the way, it is helpful for parents to join a few of their child's therapy sessions to create understanding, enable them to hear about their child's long-suppressed anger, bring comfort and support, allay their anxieties and fears, and develop a shared knowledge of what is emerging in the therapy, as their child communicates more freely and fashions a new identity.

Kim's Story

Kim was in her junior year at a small, prestigious college in Pennsylvania when her parents brought her to my office following a near-lethal suicide attempt. When Kim entered my office, I was immediately impressed by how articulate she was, and how exhausted and scared her parents looked. With them in the room, she began to tell us the details of her preparations to commit suicide. There was literally no emotion in her voice. She spoke in a flat monotone, which really gave me the chills.

Kim recounted, "I had hiked deep into a wooded park near my school with a bottle of whiskey, some clonazepam that I had stolen from a friend, and a vial of over-the-counter sleeping pills. I chugged the alcohol while swallowing the pills, curled up next to a tree, and mentally prepared myself to die. Sometime later, the police found me wandering in a shopping center parking lot. Apparently I was extremely confused and disoriented and the cops assumed that I was high on drugs. Somehow, I managed to provide them my parents' phone number."

Her parents were awakened by the call and alarmed by what they heard about her condition; as far as they knew, she had never used drugs before. They drove to campus—about three hours away—and picked Kim up. They drove back home, where Kim immediately fell asleep. Twenty-four hours later, she awoke from her stupor and told them what she had done. Frightened, they arranged for an emergency appointment with me that same day.

Kim went on. "I picked a location deep in the woods, far from any path traveled by students or joggers, to be certain that I would be successful."

As she spoke, I was scared by her story. It was a miracle she had survived; her plan had been quite lethal. I wondered whether, at some future time, I would awaken one morning to the story of her untimely death, a thought that made me feel so sad for her and wish to rescue her. These countertransference feelings of mine were based on some of my own childhood wishes to be rescued and helped me empathize with Kim.

I said, "Kim, it's likely that you are feeling an enormous amount of emotional pain in your life and have been feeling hopeless that your pain would ever go away. When you entered that wooded area, you may have felt really scared, all alone, and that there was no way out other than what you had planned. You may also have felt that relief was finally at hand, believing that your emotions, which felt so unbearable, would soon be extinguished. At some point, when you feel ready, I hope we can talk about what you were actually feeling and be able to put it into perspective, to help you learn how to feel better and find a better solution to cope with all of your feelings. You went into the woods to end what felt like an intolerable, endless pain. I promise you that if you stay alive and work really hard with me, we will figure this out. You will feel a lot better about yourself and your life. Can you tell me some more about what has been going on with you?"

While she was speaking, I was struck by the fact that her mother appeared intoxicated and would slur some of her words when it was her turn to speak. Was her intoxication a momentary lapse, an effort to cope with this terrible crisis, or did it represent a more pervasive pattern of alcohol or drug abuse? Time would tell. Kim's father, dressed in what looked like an expensive Italian suit, held himself very stiffly throughout the session and said little. He appeared bewildered and frightened.

At the end of our initial meeting, Kim agreed to come back again the next day. She would see me in intensive outpatient therapy twice a week while taking a leave of absence from college. We also agreed that her parents would join our sessions at least once a month, given that she would be living at home for the next semester. They expressed an eagerness to understand what had happened and how to prevent it from happening again and were anxious about Kim's living at home under their rules. Because she was no longer actively suicidal and because her parents were in agreement with the plan, we ended the session.

The next day, Kim returned and began to tell her story.

"Despite my record of outward accomplishments in school and athletics, inside myself, I have experienced a deep melancholia for as far back as I can remember. I have hidden many of these feelings and troubles from my parents. Their ability to understand me is questionable at best, and I can never be sure of their reactions."

She described her father as extremely accomplished, rising up from dire poverty to become the successful founder and owner of a technology company.

"However," she continued, "he is emotionally unapproachable, prone to lecturing about values and the need to 'tough it out,' as he puts it, when I am faced with adversity. I know that he loves me and that his intense professional drive is fed by a desire to provide our family with the best of everything in life. And yet I could never imagine talking with him about my feelings. He is simply not emotionally safe."

Her mother was someone who Kim loved at times and loathed at other times.

"She is chronically anxious and prone to bouts of depression," Kim said. "She drinks alcohol to excess from time to time and takes narcotic painkillers when she is severely stressed. I find it difficult to respect her. In contrast, when times are good, she can be loving and attentive."

As we came to learn more, it appeared that Kim's mother was

missing something inside. For example, Kim described how her mother reveled in Kim's athletic and academic accomplishments:

"She brags loudly about me to family friends," she said, "which has always humiliated me."

We came to understand this as her mother's efforts to fill herself up, to deal with a persisting sadness inside. What was this all about?

"My older sister suffers from schizophrenia and has received special love, attention, and schooling for as far back as I can remember. Although I have tried to be understanding about her special needs, I sometimes resent her. Despite my efforts to please both of my parents, I am alone and emotionally isolated in my home. Only my ability to perform seems to please them, to warrant their affection."

In addition, despite her love of literature and history, Kim felt that her father pressured her to become a physician or attorney, career paths that she would despise. Her dream was to become an anthropology professor by eventually earning a PhD.

"Thank you, Kim, for being this open with me so early in our relationship. You probably have so much to talk about, and I am here to listen, understand, and support. You don't need to feel so alone anymore. We'll figure this out together. I'll help you find better ways to deal with your relationship with your parents and with yourself and to feel much better. It is going to be hard work, but you are pretty used to that, aren't you?" With that, she cracked a big smile. "Kim, would you be able to tell me more about when you first began to feel so bad and what was going on in your life at that time?"

"I have become increasingly disconsolate over the last five years, maybe longer. I have always feared informing my parents about it. I was apprehensive that not only would I disappoint them, but I would add to the burden they already feel in caring for my sister. I believe the downslide began when I lost my star status on the lacrosse field. In middle school, I was the captain of the lacrosse team, played on an elite traveling team, and was very popular and sought after by many of the boys. In high school, my life began to turn upside down: Some of my team members were more outstanding, and I was mainly benched during the games. I also developed acne, especially on my face. I felt ugly and was no longer considered one of the popular kids, who I began to hold in disdain. I then went through an existential phase in my junior and senior years of high school, feeling that life was absurd and pointless. I began to stop caring about just about everything."

I felt sad for her, given the losses she had sustained and her painful self-consciousness. I also recalled how I felt at that age, with rampant acne and no longer a track star, as other boys were maturing much faster than me.

This countertransference response led me to say, "Kim, feeling depressed over losing the prestige and status that came from being a valued player and captain of your lacrosse team and then feeling upset over your physical appearance is entirely understandable. It is not uncommon to feel self-hatred and even self-loathing at those times. To make matters worse, you felt that you couldn't talk with your parents about your feelings, which left you feeling pretty much all alone. In addition to the depression, were you also feeling anger and bitterness over what was happening? What did you do with those feelings?"

She hesitated, then revealed, "When I felt the most self-loathing, I would secretly cut myself on my arms or thighs, which temporarily relieved the horrible feelings inside."

Following this disclosure, Kim began to develop a greater attachment to me and our work together. On one occasion, she told me that she wished that I was her father; this was a transference reaction, her seeing me as a caring paternal figure.

Despite her struggles, Kim became a varsity athlete, was an honor student succeeding in AP classes, and applied to a number of the finer colleges and universities. She ultimately attended the small, elite college in Pennsylvania that her mother most favored, instead of the larger university in the Deep South that Kim had felt was best for her.

"Once I was in college," she said, "I began drinking heavily at frat parties with friends who would ultimately become my sorority sisters. We sought blackout sex, and I engaged in a number of meaningless hookups and spiraled into deeper depression. My classroom attendance began to wane, and I began failing several courses."

And then there was that fateful evening when, filled with so much despair following a frat party where she once again got drunk and hooked up, terrified to tell her parents that she was failing out of college. "I took that bottle of whiskey, the stolen clonazepam, and the sleeping pills and entered the woods, prepared to die."

There was a long pause at this point; we both realized the enormity of what she was feeling at that moment. We looked at each other; her eyes began to fill with tears, and so did mine. I tried to look at her in a caring and loving way and tried to communicate nonverbally that I understood how much emotional pain she was feeling. Then I actively empathized with how deep and prolonged her emotional pain had been and with how alone she had felt for so many years:

"It is so terribly sad that you felt that pain and despair for so long, Kim, and that you felt you could not reveal it to anyone and had to carry such a huge burden all by yourself and felt so alone. I'm really glad that you're telling me all of this now and hope that I can help shoulder some of your burden. I know I can help you to figure out some solutions to how bad you have been feeling about your life and yourself so that you can feel better soon."

In response, she openly sobbed, with a torrent of tears that had been building up for years, saying, "I have felt so terribly alone, for such a long time!" At that moment, I really wished that I could give her a big hug, just to comfort her, but that's not how therapy works.

It was apparent that Kim was quite depressed, and so we initiated antidepressant medication therapy. She also tested positive on an assessment for ADHD (predominantly inattentive type), and so we began treatment with stimulant medication as well. Kim began to feel better from these medications and our talks.

Over the ensuing months, Kim came twice a week to therapy, and we formed an excellent therapeutic alliance.[3] Not infrequently, we would share music that would elicit deeply held feelings in her. As she recounted her life, she shared memories filled with disappointment in her parents that they had placed so much pressure on her to achieve, anger that they had favored her sister, and contempt for her mother's episodic drinking and drug abuse. I gradually balanced an empathetic approach with interpretations of her parents' behaviors in the context of their own childhood and adult struggles. I helped Kim understand that her mother was a lonely woman whose own mother was cold and unempathic and that the challenges of raising a schizophrenic child were daunting.

"I have begun to feel proud of my mother's efforts on behalf of my sister," Kim said. "My sister has progressed from having serious interpersonal limitations to enjoying a social life, being able to attend community college, and successfully living in an apartment with a roommate—all largely as a result of my mother's persistent diligence in locating the best resources to help her overcome her disabilities."

While living at home, Kim began to approach her father and open up more to him after she appreciated the hardships he overcame in lifting himself out of poverty to achieve his financial success. She came to understand how he had needed to suppress his own emotions to drive himself to succeed against the odds.

Throughout these months, Kim attended a local community college and obtained straight A's while working in a retail clothing store. She was well behaved at home, and we all concluded that she was ready to return to living away at college in the fall. It turned out that our confidence in Kim was quite misplaced, given subsequent developments. Those initial feelings of fear for her life that I had felt in our first session together were about to return.

Kim returned to campus after much careful planning. We discussed and established that she would live with emotionally stable and academically serious roommates who valued hard work and abstinence from alcohol and drugs. She agreed to drop out of her sorority, cease attending fraternity parties, and maintain a part-time job at a retail store near campus. She worked out an arrangement with the dean's office to switch her major to anthropology, because she had a passion for it and wanted to teach it. Her parents were in full support. We agreed to continue our weekly psychotherapy sessions by videoconference, and Kim agreed to meet every other week with a counselor at the college's Office of Disability Services (ODS) to learn how to implement routines that would enable her to successfully manage her academic responsibilities. Separately, I arranged for routine coordination among the ODS, her professors, the dean's office, and me. The dean's office was to call me if Kim missed any of the counseling sessions with ODS or if she skipped any classes.

During our weekly video sessions, Kim assured me that "All is well. I am fully committed to following this plan. You and my parents need to stop worrying about me. I have my life under control now."

I later discovered that she was lying; she had fallen through a hole in the safety net we had created. I was shocked and disappointed to learn that the dean's office had failed to monitor and report Kim's lack of attendance in class and at the ODS. The real story eventually emerged, and it was highly disturbing.

Six weeks into the semester, about four weeks after Kim unilaterally decided to stop taking her medication, she got into a shouting match with some drunken students who had hurled racial epithets at Kim's boyfriend while he and she were taking a walk. The students physically attacked her, and she fell to the ground and struck her head. Kim suffered a brief loss of consciousness and, when she awoke, felt dazed and confused. Her boyfriend dialed 911, and Kim was taken to the local emergency room, where she was diagnosed with a concussion.

At the time, Kim didn't call me to tell me what had happened to her. In our therapy session two days later, I noticed she was speaking slowly and slurring her words, but when I asked her about it, she refused to tell me why. Unaware of her mild traumatic brain injury, I was concerned that she had begun using drugs again and felt scared for her, afraid that she might slide back into that abyss that almost took her life.

I asked her, "Kim, have you started to use alcohol or drugs again?" She denied it.

I confronted her: "Kim, it's really important that you be open and honest with me. Something is not right with you. We have been through a lot together, so please tell me what is going on."

She quickly became angry. "Why would you accuse me of lying? This is exactly what my father would do!" This was another example of transference, this time of negative feelings. "I should find another doctor, never speak with you again. I have been studying very hard and not sleeping well; this is why I don't sound like my usual self."

Instinctively, I didn't believe her, and I felt disturbed by the fact that I knew something was up and that Kim was concealing it.

From my unconscious mind, a memory emerged from long ago, when a relative overdosed on drugs and died. I recalled the pain that my family had gone through and was determined that this would not happen to Kim, her family and friends (or me) if I could help it.

I immediately called her counselor at ODS (having previously secured Kim's written permission to speak with him) and learned that not only was Kim failing to attend sessions at the ODS, but she was also skipping her classes again. Clearly, Kim was in decline, and my fears heightened. I had to get to the bottom of what was going on with her—but how?

Kim called me the next day, terrified that something was seriously wrong with her.

"I can't seem to remember anything, and I'm stumbling each time I try to walk."

Angrily, I said to her, "Kim, you need to tell me what is going on! Your life may be in danger here!"

She finally revealed what had happened when she was assaulted, and I recommended that we call her parents to have them immediately drive to Philadelphia and be at her side to help her.

"Absolutely not!" she protested. "I am over eighteen, so you have to respect my wishes not to notify them. I will handle this on my own."

We quickly arranged for her to have an emergency MRI of the head, which fortunately showed no bleeding or overt brain damage. She saw a consulting neurologist, who confirmed the earlier diagnosis of concussion and that Kim's condition had not worsened.

I breathed a sigh of relief, because this explained her ominous behavior. The acute crisis was resolving, but there were additional steps necessary. First and foremost, I was finally able to convince Kim to call her parents and tell them what had happened. Alarmed, they immediately dropped everything and traveled to the campus. Her parents were surprisingly supportive, and together, we worked out an arrangement with the dean to have Kim drop two courses and continue attending school part time. Her post-concussion syndrome with lingering cognitive symptoms made it impossible to manage a full course load. She again agreed to the weekly counseling sessions at ODS. The situation was finally moving in a positive direction, and I was feeling hopeful again.

During some moments of quiet reflection, I felt angry and betrayed by Kim (my negative countertransference toward her). Despite what

I had believed to be a strong bond of trust between us, she had lied to me, conned me into thinking she would follow the treatment plan we had designed together. Managing these feelings was challenging. I recalled how scary it was when I first learned about Kim's fateful walk into those woods. I wondered whether I really knew her at all. After careful consideration, I shared with her my disappointment and anger over this betrayal and then explored with her why she felt the need to conceal from me what was really going on and why she abandoned our treatment plan without informing me.

"Your disappointment and anger surprise me," she said, "as does the fact that you would share those feelings with me. It makes me think you care, that you're not just a paid shrink—in it for the money.

"I feared being completely honest with you from the start. I felt the treatment plan you had designed was excessive and parts of it unnecessary, and I believed you would have summarily dismissed my objections and told me that you would no longer treat me. I didn't want you to abandon me."

Her transference feelings were not based in reality, and so I clarified: "Kim, your feelings are very important to me, and I would really prefer that you share them, rather than act them out by not telling me the truth. I would never abandon you for expressing your feelings. We will work together to establish a treatment plan acceptable to both of us, that will bring us the confidence that you have the best possible prospects for feeling better and moving forward."

She said, "I think I confused you with my parents, with whom my feelings haven't seemed to matter much over the years. Thank you for not abandoning me. I'm sorry for not telling you the truth; I will try to tell you everything important from now on."

I really wanted to believe her, but an inner voice warned me to proceed with caution as she had been so secretive. I felt that there was still something she wasn't telling me—some barrier between us that kept her from being completely honest. . . .

Kim continued to recover slowly and returned home for winter break, seemingly closer to her parents than ever before. It turned out to be the calm before the storm. The second night after she returned home, Kim opened up to her mother about some of the issues that we had been discussing in treatment—for example, how, for years, she had admired her father yet had felt emotionally estranged from him and had longed to feel close to him and be "Daddy's little girl." After several hours of conversation, she went into her bedroom and tried to fall asleep. She then overheard her mother picking a fight with her father, berating him over what Kim had shared with her.

Feeling despondent that her confidence had been violated and hopeless that her relationship with her parents would ever improve, Kim grabbed the keys to one of the family cars and took off, heading north toward her boyfriend, who was still at school.

Several hours later, she called me.

"I'm standing on an embankment," she said soberly. "I am going to jump over the side and drown myself in the river below. I can't take any more betrayals or emotional pain. It feels so overwhelming again, just like when I walked into the woods."

I felt really scared; it was easy enough for Kim to jump into the water and be killed on impact or be carried away to her death by the current. I felt furious with her mother for violating Kim's trust and showing such a lack of judgment. I was glad that Kim had called me prior to jumping, and as all of this was flashing through my mind, I struggled with what I would say to her next. What would bring her back from the brink of destruction?

"Kim, I am really glad that you reached out to me. Please stay on the line and hear me out. What your mother did was wrong. She violated a confidence you had placed in her, yet perhaps her heart was in a good place, in taking your side and somehow trying to defend or support you with your father. You know how she panics sometimes and gets impulsive. This is one of those times. Unlike the past, your parents are now willing to sit and listen to you. It is not hopeless like it once was. They are really trying to understand. Give them that opportunity to be there for you and listen to your disappointment and anger over this. Please don't do anything to harm yourself. I promise that I am here as your friend, ally, and doctor and that, together, we can work this through."

For over an hour, I implored Kim to come back to her parents' home, told her that I was genuinely hopeful for her life improving and that I would arrange for an emergency family session to work out these issues. She noted that her parents had refused to attend a number of the family sessions in the past, but I convinced her that it was different this time; they had learned how to listen to her emotional pain, albeit responding at times in clumsy and unhelpful ways, as her mother had just done.

Finally, to my great relief, Kim agreed to return home. The next afternoon, we met for an emergency family session, and it was "open season on Dr. Bruce." Both of her parents scathingly criticized me, saying that I had failed to treat her according to accepted medical standards, that I had overprescribed medication, that I had neglected to notify them of her concussion, and that they were going to pull her out of treatment and consider "other options" with respect to dealing with me, including consulting with their attorney.

Although it was not the outcome I had hoped for, at least they were not attacking Kim. Out of fear, they were blaming me instead. Better that I be the target than their daughter, although sitting there and enduring their withering attack had me sweating through my clothing. I began to get a feeling for what Kim had endured with them in the past, and it was pretty ugly.

Then her parents abruptly ended the session, got up from their seats, and walked out of the office with Kim in tow. She glanced back at me with a look of helplessness, bewilderment, and fear. I was in turmoil over how to salvage her treatment and help her reclaim her life.

The next day, I reached out to her parents by telephone, and they refused to return my call. When I spoke with Kim, she informed me that "my parents decline to speak with you. They have insisted that I seek treatment with a new psychiatrist. There is nothing that you or I can do to change their decision. It is final."

I heard nothing from Kim or her parents for the next six months. Then, one day out of the blue, she called me. I was happy to hear from her but felt quite guarded.

"I'm living in an off-campus apartment," she said, "working at a specialty grocery store. I am emotionally stable, clean and sober, and have met a new boyfriend who is a stabilizing influence in my life. I would like to resume our sessions if you would take me back."

Although her parents refused to pay for any treatment with me, she had saved enough money for a few sessions and asked for my assistance in working with the dean's office to get her reinstated. I agreed to help her for a substantially reduced fee, and we worked out a Hail Mary plan approved by the dean, who pointed out that this would be Kim's last chance. I felt a sense of elation that she was still alive and wanted my help in moving on with her life.

According to the plan, Kim was to be strictly monitored during weekly sessions with the school's counseling staff, who would also remain in weekly contact with her professors. She was barred from attending frat parties, and if she was found to violate this provision, she would be immediately expelled from the school. She also agreed to attend three twelve-step programs per week for additional support and relapse prevention. During the course of this process, Kim told me that her parents had relented and agreed to support ongoing therapy with me, given how helpful I had been in getting her reinstated.

"I feel healthy and stable," Kim said, when she began her fall semester classes. "I am exercising regularly, and my boyfriend also keeps a watchful eye over me."

We had survived another crisis and were settling in to this next phase of work together.

"Kim," I said, "I feel so proud of you. You negotiated this complex transition without drinking or using drugs and have worked with your parents, the dean, and me in such a constructive fashion."

About four weeks later, she missed one of our therapy sessions and failed to return my phone calls. Finally, in response to a letter I sent to her, she called and said, "I no longer want treatment from you. I will receive it through the school's counseling center. My parents insist on finding another doctor."

"Would the three of you consider discussing this decision with me in a family therapy session?" I asked.

"No. We just want a new beginning with a new doctor. Coming to see you would just bring back too many painful memories for all of us."

I felt heartbroken. We had worked so hard to get through so much together, Kim finally appeared to be turning a corner, and I selfishly wanted to be around for all of the good things that would likely follow.

Although I believed in my heart that it would be helpful for Kim and her parents to work through these issues with me, I respected their decision. Kim had adopted one of her father's defense mechanisms of soldiering on without recognizing or working through deeply held feelings. I concluded that this was what she needed at this phase of her life, and that a positive identification with her father's adaptive style might bring her closer to him, which was certainly a positive development, given how alone she had felt in her family for so many years.

"Thank you for all of the help you have provided me," she said.

"Kim, therapy is usually properly terminated by taking a few sessions to say goodbye and to review what we have accomplished. Would you be willing to end our relationship in this way?"

She simply said, "No."

"Okay," I continued. "My door is always open should you wish to see me again. Good luck, Kim. I wish you well."

From time to time, I think about her and wonder how she is faring in life.

Kim's demons had been hiding inside of her for a number of years, finally breaking out on that fateful day when she walked into the woods to die. They occasionally reemerged during the course of her therapy. It is all too easy to fall back into an existential crisis when making the years-long transition from child to adult, but doing so under the care of a well-trained therapist can help ease the emotional pain.

Begin to Heal

If you are the parent of a late teen or young adult child in significant emotional distress and they are about to leave for college or have already matriculated, I have a number of ideas to impart to you. To begin with, it is understandable if you feel anxious about their transitioning from a sheltered and highly structured home and school life to a culture where, for the first time, they are completely responsible for their day-to-day life—all the more so when you feel out of touch with what they are going through, and their distress is palpable. Take some comfort in the fact that millions of kids have successfully navigated this large step toward independence, but expect that they will encounter bumps in the road that may require your assistance. It is my hope that the following steps outlined below will give you the tools you need to provide that assistance as effectively as possible. Some of them will involve self-reflection regarding your parenting style and asking yourself some tough questions in the service of taking responsibility for mistakes you may have made—and doing a better job in the future. Please keep in mind that none of us is a perfect parent and that, even if your heart is in a good place, introspection can assist you in becoming a more effective parent. Please take out your workbook to write down your responses to the following prompts and questions:

Step 1: Reflect on your parenting.

Take time to reflect on your own child-rearing style, and be willing to acknowledge the good, the bad, and the ugly. In what areas of your child's life do you feel proud of your parenting? Are there other areas of their life where you overreact? Is your behavior reminiscent of one or both of your parents? List some of the triggers to your exaggerated response. How might you handle these situations more effectively?

Step 2: Consider your motivation (whose life is it anyway?).

Are you pushing your child into pursuits that don't really interest them? Rather than force your passions on your child—whether in music, sports, or scholarship—encourage them to explore their own passions. And be supportive when these change (as they invariably will), even if your star soccer player decides to give it up to try lacrosse and it represents a loss for you because you used to play soccer! What would ignite *their* passion? How might you come to feel good about it?

Step 3: Put yourself in their shoes.

To empathize more effectively, try to recall what it was like when you were the same age. What were the challenges in your life at that time? What did you want? What would you have wished for from your parents, to help you feel better and cope more effectively? A note of caution: We unconsciously assume that our child is facing the same challenges that we did, that they are like a little me (or you), but their challenges are never identical to what we faced growing up. This part can be really tough to figure out. Many parents work hard to fill in voids from their own childhood instead of providing what's missing from their child's. Here are some of the warning signs of narcissistically loving your child:

- You are *too* emotionally invested in their accomplishments.

- Your self-esteem rises and falls with their achievements. (Your children shouldn't be used to solve your own unhappiness; that is too great a burden for them to bear—and, in any event, that is your job.)

- You assume that their wants, needs, and goals in life are similar to your own.

- Your hopes and dreams for them exceed their abilities to deliver (this particularly comes out in the areas of school and athletic performance).

- You reveal inappropriate aspects of your personal life to them (e.g., your unhappiness with your spouse).

- You disparage your spouse in front of them.

- Your child repeatedly chooses pleasing you over figuring out what will make them happy (e.g., the extracurricular activities they pursue, the college they choose to attend).

- You talk over them or tell them how they should feel.

- You share your feelings of anxiety or depression with them.

- You are intoxicated in front of them.

- You openly fight with your spouse, as opposed to taking these conflicts behind closed doors or to a couples therapist.

Step 4: Communicate your emotional support.

Let your child know that you are there to support and help them during this time of great transition and that they should not be afraid to report to you when they have done something they feel is stupid or shameful or that you would be angry about. Reassure them that you will not abandon or harshly judge them but will, instead, be constructive in finding a solution. Will this be difficult to discuss with them? If so, what gets in the way? How might you remove the obstacles?

Step 5: Pay attention to changes in your child's behavior.

Has your child become withdrawn, sullen, or persistently angry? Have they become more introverted and less involved with friends and in school activities? Are they showing symptoms of insomnia, a decline in school grades, rule-breaking behavior, spending much more time in their bedroom, having crying spells, and quitting sports teams or after-school activities that they previously enjoyed? Write down any and all observations that describe these changes and the associated timeline for each. What are some of the possible triggers for what you are observing in them? What life experiences may be contributing? The answers to these questions will help you empathize with their plight and feel less scared and confused.

Step 6: What's happening at school?

If your child is still in high school and two or more of these behavioral changes are present, contact their school and ask to speak with teachers or coaches to see if they have noticed any changes and, if so, when it began. Prepare a list of questions to ask them beforehand.

Step 7: Contact their friends.

If your child attends college and is unwilling to speak with you about your concerns, and you have a good relationship with one or more of your child's close friends, reach out to them to see if they are concerned. What are they observing? Tell them you don't want them to reveal any confidences but that you are worried and want to help. Your inquiry and offer of support may alleviate a somewhat frightening burden that their friends are shouldering.

Step 8: Choose their therapist carefully.

In selecting a professional to evaluate and treat your child, choose one whose treatment style includes parental involvement. It does not make sense to have your child living at home and treated in isolation from family dynamics that contribute to their depression or anxiety. What are some of the possible family dynamics that are tangling up your child's life? Please write them down here to present to the therapist.

Step 9: Take action.

It is important that your child's condition be promptly evaluated before it worsens to a crisis point. Early intervention is the key to preventing suicide attempts and accelerating the recovery process. The more embedded the depression becomes, the longer it will take to effectively treat it, and the higher the risk of dangerous behavior. Are you reluctant to have your child seek treatment? If so, why? Who have you spoken with about this, and what do they think?

Are feelings of shame or embarrassment in the way? What are you afraid of? Writing out the answers to these questions can help you overcome concerns about this important next step.

Step 10: Maintain continuity in their therapy.

If your child has been treated for a mood, anxiety, or substance-abuse disorder and they are about to return to college or enroll for the first time, arrange for them to continue treatment with their current therapist by telephone or video conference. This is particularly helpful during this time of transition if they have a significant bond with the therapist. If there is not much of an attachment, arrange for them to be referred to a professional in the college town. Names can be obtained from the dean's office, Student Health, or the office of disability services.

Step 11: Plan for the transition.

Ask your child to interview with a few professionals until they find one with whom they feel a good initial fit. If they are on prescription medication, arrange to have new prescriptions written to take to the local pharmacy near their school, or have their psychiatrist call in the medications by phone. Pack an extra supply of a month or two of these medications just in case there is a problem transferring them to the local pharmacy. Some parents continue to fill the prescriptions locally and mail or FedEx them to their child, if this is more reliable or convenient.

Step 12: Gather local contacts.

When you travel with your child to move them into their dormitory room, introduce yourself to their roommate and obtain contact information for them and their parents, including mobile telephone numbers and email addresses. In the future, if you have difficulty reaching your child, these contacts will enable you to find out what is going on.

Step 13: Communicate your approval.

Let your child know how proud you are of them and that you love and admire them for their hard work and diligence. Let them know that you will always be there for them—no matter what—for emotional support and guidance.

Step 14: Trust, but verify.

Let them know that you don't want to infringe on their independence, but you expect regular communication with them—at least once a week—and you want to establish a regular time for this (e.g., Sunday evenings). Skype and FaceTime are wonderful technologies that will enable you to feel that you are in your child's dorm room with them during the weekly calls.

Step 15: Let go.

Don't interfere with a high-school romance that appears to continue after your child leaves for college. Although it is understandable that you may want them to break off this relationship to fully experience campus life, you should not force this issue. A high-school sweetheart can serve as a transitional object to provide comfort and support to your child at a time of high anxiety as they separate from home.

This is undoubtedly an anxious time for you, something we'll address in more detail in the next chapter. An existential crisis in a young adult is scary: The child that you thought you knew appears to have disappeared, and you may experience a great sense of loss along with fears that they will never recover. With therapy, and the patient pursuit of understanding by family members, your child will emerge stronger, with a more authentic sense of self, a clearer understanding of what will bring them satisfaction in life, and an identity that feels more true to them than the earlier identity that was based on pleasing others.

Self-Help Steps for Young Adults

If you have a child suffering through an existential crisis, I urge you to share the following steps with them. These prompts and questions will help them through this turbulent time, allow them to gain a clearer understanding of what they're suffering through, and remind them that they're not alone in this struggle. Encourage them to write their answers down in a journal.

Step 1: Connect with someone.

Although the road ahead may appear bleak or hopeless, it is vital that you not withdraw and become isolated. Is there someone in your life who you trust? Who? Do you have a friend, parent, aunt or uncle, grandparent, or teacher you could open up your heart to? What would you say to them? Write out your thoughts and feelings. What's most important is to select someone you feel comfortable with, who is a good listener, and is nonjudgmental. It's okay if they don't know you so well, as long as they are willing to give you the time you need to tell your story and unburden yourself. You want someone who will also be willing to listen to you time and again, who is patient, caring, loving, and truly wants the best for you. You may be afraid to share your true feelings with them; perhaps they have come to know you as a driven high achiever and you fear letting them down. It's okay to feel those fears, just don't let them hold you back from being open and honest about how you really feel.

Step 2: Make thoughtful decisions.

You may want to withdraw from school for a semester or even a year, feeling that it is no longer right for you. This idea may be really scary, because you have been driven to excel in school for years, yet no longer feel that drive inside of you. Write down all of the pluses and minuses related to this decision. How would you spend your time each day if you were not attending school? It is not a good idea to just sit at home. What are your options? What about a full-time job? Who has openings near your home? What about a part-time job and attending a few classes at a local community college while you figure things out? What are the pluses and minuses of living at home for a while? What rules would you be willing to accept while living under your parents' roof? The decision to take time off from school should be discussed with close and trusted friends, parents, and others who have been deeply involved in your life.

Step 3: Seek professional help.

Are you open to seeking professional help? If not, why not? What would be your goals for treatment? Which symptoms trouble you the most? What are the major life issues that need to be untangled? Which patterns of behavior have you repeated over and over that no longer work for you? Psychotherapy and medication may rapidly reverse symptoms of depression and trouble concentrating, so you may want to put off taking a leave of absence until you see how the treatment makes you feel.

Step 4: Determine your emotional state.

Do you feel that you have enough emotional strength to wait and see how you fare in treatment, or is it essential that you have immediate relief from the pressures of school? Write out your thoughts and feelings as you answer this important question.

Step 5: Enter treatment immediately.

If you decide that a medical withdrawal from school is the right decision, it is vital that you enter treatment shortly after you arrive back home. Which doctors might you interview shortly after you arrive back home? What are the qualities of the doctor that are most important to you? Are you willing to ask your parents for help in selecting candidates to treat you? If not, why? Who else might you ask for assistance in locating the best doctor for you?

Step 6: Engage with the world.

Once you return home, being engaged in the outside world is crucial; it will help you fend off the longing to withdraw out of feelings of shame and depression. Staying at home, locked away in your bedroom, will only serve to worsen your despair and deepen your depression. If you feel too ill to work or attend community college, is there somewhere you might volunteer? Is there a cause you really believe in that might need your help on a part-time basis? Is there a gym near your home that you might join for regular workouts to help you feel better? Is there a former teacher or coach you might connect with who would share a coffee with you from time to time, just to talk? Who?

Step 7: Get to know your true self.

You may well feel that you have been living a lie for much of your life, and that can feel really scary as well. The person that you have known yourself to be up until recently no longer seems to make sense or even exist, and it can be terrifying to realize that, for now, you have no recognizable identity. It may feel that you have lost what has anchored you to life. What aspects of yourself still seem real and true? Write them out. Which relationships in your life still bring meaning and purpose? Who are the people that help you feel better about yourself? How might you engage with them on a more regular basis? Can you hang out together? Are there common interests that might be shared? Try to focus on those around you who love you and who are willing to listen, and gain comfort from them.

Step 8: Be patient with yourself.

Try to see this as a temporary crisis, from which you will develop an identity that you fully own—one that feels authentic. Discovering that identity will be one of the principal goals of your therapy and your discussions with those who love you. Find a psychiatrist or therapist that you like and respect—one that is easy to talk to. Allow them to involve your parents in your treatment, because the road ahead will be bumpy and filled with huge potholes, and it can be helpful if your parents have confidence in your doctor and the treatment plan. You don't want them to be in the dark, or to have their anxieties or fears make you feel even worse.

Step 9: Be open and honest in therapy.

Be certain to tell your therapist anything and everything that comes into your mind once you trust them. Full disclosure, even when the issue feels shameful or humiliating, will help to ease your feelings of aloneness and will facilitate understanding yourself more deeply when you feel so confused. What do you think will be the most difficult issues for you to face in therapy? Please write them out here. What will you be afraid of in bringing them up? What are your fantasies about what will happen if you do?

Step 10: Persist. Believe in yourself.

Stick with the therapy to fully untangle your heart and become whole. If you feel at some point that therapy is not helping, discuss this openly with your therapist. If it feels too emotionally painful and overwhelming, ask for extra support in the form of medication and additional sessions. The goal is to stabilize your condition and to alleviate your depression and difficulty concentrating so that you can use the therapy more effectively to figure out what you really want and need for yourself and what will make you happy. If you stick with it, I promise you that, over time, you will feel less chaotic inside and will begin to consolidate a new identity that feels stronger.

* * *

We have been talking a lot about children and how to assist them in their growth and development, preparing them for the adult world, and trying to ensure that their emotional maturation has evolved to the point where they successfully launch into adulthood. You have been working hard, and I really appreciate your efforts. In our next session together, we will explore what it feels like to let go of your child as they become more independent and its impact on your stage of life and on your marriage or life partner. I hope to see you soon.

SESSION SIX

Let Go of Your Child as They Become an Adult

For those of you with a child entering young adulthood, it may be a bittersweet time characterized by both sadness and loss as they leave your home. It may also be a time of hope and excitement as your child launches into that next phase of life. It may bring you a newfound emotional freedom in your day-to-day life.

It is one of the more challenging epochs if you are the type of parent who is actively and lovingly engaged in your child's emotional growth and development. As a parent, having your child graduate into adulthood emotionally healthy and independent is a source of great pride and personal satisfaction—and, of course, brings with it a feeling of tremendous relief! There are numerous issues and bumps in the road that arise along this phase of the shared journey. Many relate to the dynamic tension that arises as your child begins to assert their independence and the inevitable experiences that disappoint, that fall short of the dreams that we held for them, or that they dreamed for themselves.

How do we simultaneously let go and remain involved and engaged at a level where our child feels adequately supported, without undermining their independence and the confidence that comes from tackling the challenges of the outside world and progressively mastering them? How do we tolerate the emotional pain that comes along with the process of letting go, while accepting a diminished role in our child's life? How do we endure the ups and downs of their simultaneously abandoning us and excessively asserting themselves against us? How do we prevent feeling like an outmoded dinosaur and remain relevant and important to them in new ways?

♪ **Session Soundtrack** ♪

"Child's Song," by Tom Rush, is a touching story of a child who is about to leave home. He is speaking to his parents and sister as he packs up to leave, and his words touch on a number of the themes and emotional challenges of this stage of life as he says goodbye to them, to the house where he grew up, and to all of the memories that it holds. In these lyrics, issues such as parental overprotectiveness, the meaning of getting older for both the child and the parent, and what the younger sibling will face in the coming years are all touched on. They speak to a child who is, at once, sensitive and rebellious, expressing his love and gratitude while distancing himself emotionally as he prepares to leave for good.

Visit DrBruceKehr.com/music-5 for audio files
and further discussion of the soundtracks.

There are no easy answers to these questions. Our children at this phase of their lives are going through a phase of separation and individuation. In this phase, they solidify an adult identity, choose a career path, and engage in more-mature love relationships, eventually settling on a mate. This process takes place over a period of years and rarely occurs without setbacks. The challenge we face as parents is to let go yet remain engaged, perhaps recalling what it felt like to be young and scared as we ourselves once entered this phase of our journey. At times, it means sitting back and passively observing our child's inevitable mistakes and lack of judgment as they engage with the real world, only stepping in when we believe serious harm is about to take place.

There is a lot to contemplate and live through for both child and parent, including the child's search for meaning and purpose, their desire to get away from home and explore, and anxieties about whether they will find an identity that fits them well. At a time of such great uncertainty, a book that may bring comfort to your young adult is Tina Seelig's *What I Wish I Knew When I Was 20*.

For many parents, letting go of their child and trusting that they will safely make their way, exercise good judgment, make the right decisions, stay out of trouble, and not commit huge blunders is an anxiety-provoking prospect. A parent may yearn for an earlier phase when life was much simpler and they felt a sense of control over their child's life and the power to protect, nurture, and encourage. In this new phase, "If only they would listen to me" may become a familiar refrain as your child repudiates your advice (at times, only to turn around and accept the same advice from one of their friends!).

Your child must find their own path through life. It is not a road that you can—or should—determine for them. Our children develop wisdom through life experience; it is not something that we can pass on to them. Through experiencing and overcoming emotionally painful disappointments and losses, they become more adept at managing adult-world challenges. When we try to offer our wisdom, it may well be ignored or discounted, and it can drive them away. Well, then, if we can't provide the benefits of our wisdom, how can we effectively parent and simultaneously let go? This is the question I hope to answer in this session.

Although not every story has a happy ending, most children solidify an adult identity, create a career path, and build a life with someone they love. This process may take up to a decade or more, particularly in today's increasingly complicated and fast-moving world. For you and your partner, your child's emergence into adulthood will bring a newfound freedom and a great sense of relief. Letting go can facilitate a more loving relationship as you give back love to one another. And keep in mind that, as your child settles into a new life, putting into practice what you have taught them, you will have the opportunity to participate in their lives in a new way, watching them grow, develop, and change. They will continue to need your love and support. Although it may feel that way at first, you haven't lost them forever.

Alice's Story

Alice was seventeen when she was brought into my office by her parents, Randi and Tom, and in the first session, it was clear that she was extremely angry with them and had only reluctantly come to meet with me. Alice was an honors student in her junior year at a local Catholic high school, and she was taking a number of AP courses, aiming for a career in computer science. Complicating matters were her parents' religious preferences: Her mother, Randi, had been raised in a Jewish household and was now an atheist, and her father actively practiced Catholicism.

Both parents reported that Alice hated the school that she attended and that it had recently been a daily struggle to get her to go to class. She appeared to be a bright and interesting young woman but was highly reticent and painfully shy. She refused to utter a word the entire first session and let her parents monopolize the time by giving all of the background information. (This was a measure of both how angry and scared she felt and how anxious and out of control her parents were feeling.) Alice initially glared at me and then began to look down at the floor, dejected. I sensed a profound sadness emanating from her.

She was fourteen months younger than her sister, who was described as an outstanding student athlete and an obedient daughter. In contrast, Alice was described as the rebel of the two, consistently challenging and testing the rules. And her parents really hated her boyfriend, Eddie. He was a senior at her school, a superb athlete, and the star quarterback of the football team but not academically motivated. He liked to have a good time, was an average student, and was very popular. The two of them had recently cut school together, which further inflamed Alice's tensions with her parents.

"Eddie is a terrible influence on her," they said. "We've been encouraging her to break off the relationship. Alice's grades have declined since she began seeing him. We sit with her each evening while she does her homework, but she's still not improving."

Finally, they told me of a recent incident: "Alice and Eddie spent the night at a mutual friend's house, and Alice gave up her virginity." Her mother looked so sad, and her father's eyes were filled with rage and hatred.

Following this revelation, you could hear a pin drop in the room. Each moment seemed interminable. I could only imagine how much emotional pain Alice was feeling as her parents dissected and passed judgment on her private life in front of a stranger. She probably wanted to crawl into the woodwork and disappear. I looked over at her with compassion, and she looked up at me with defiance in her eyes, then looked back down at the floor. She appeared so sad and forlorn. It was going to be tough to get her to open up; she looked so uncomfortable just being there. Her embarrassment, humiliation, and anger were written all over her face.

Finally, after what seemed like an eternity—but was actually just a few seconds—I asked, "What happened next?"

Her father admitted that when he had found out, he had slapped Alice across the face. He had begun screaming at her and calling her names like "whore" and "slut." He had ranted about how she and her sister were Catholic, how she had violated their belief system, and how she had shamed the entire family.

He had then added, "If you get pregnant, you can never come home again. You will have to take care of yourself and the baby all by yourself. Your Aunt Sally got pregnant when she was in high school, and look at what a disaster her life has turned out to be!"

It was time for me to step in and address both parents and child, to relieve tension and provide some hope. Inside, I struggled with what to say to them, given how polarized Alice and her parents had become. She was struggling to separate into an independent young woman and had made some mistakes along the way. Had she learned anything from her mistakes? Time would tell. Her parents were probably terrified that Alice would shatter her (and their) future plans and dreams and had become more controlling and domineering in response, which only served to alienate her from them even more.

Her father's fear verged on paranoia, and yet, as a father myself, I could empathize with his plight. So I decided to lead with some empathetic comments to begin to build trust and credibility with each of them and to mirror what they all needed to develop: a capacity to listen to and understand one another, rather than reflexively reacting out of hurt, anger, or fear. If I could assist them in developing empathy toward one another and could help Alice express her feelings through words as opposed to acting out, in the context of an emotionally safe relationship, it would help her parents let go of her, help Alice find her voice, and support her in developing a healthier adult self. Armed with an initial game plan, I took a deep breath and began to speak.

"These events are so distressing for each of you. Perhaps you also feel confused by it all. There is so much anger and sadness here, and you don't know what to do or where to go with what you are feeling and what has happened. You may be feeling helpless and powerless and stuck in such an uncomfortable place. I'm glad you've come in to see me, and we can work hard together to figure all of this out and improve your relationships. We will untangle what has happened to your family and enable your lives to move on in a better direction."

I then thought of a way that I could begin to show Alice that I could be her friend and ally, so I said, "There have to be some ground rules if we are going to work together, and the first one is that, from now on, there will be no physical expressions of anger. Any angry feelings have to be put into words and not be the basis of violent acts. Can you all agree to this?"

Each of them nodded their head affirmatively. Even though this admonition was meant for all three of them, as I finished saying it, I looked directly at Alice's father and held my gaze on him for a few moments. He was a large man and somewhat intimidating, and it was important that Alice recognize that I was not scared by him. We would set limits on everyone's out of control behavior—not just hers.

In addition to educating all of them on the developmental challenges facing Alice, what would be involved in letting go of her, and how scared and excited she felt in moving toward a more independent life, I hoped to help Alice and her parents stop objectifying one another. Instead, I hoped they would come to learn about what each of them thought and felt and to understand the reasons behind their respective actions. In the months ahead, we would be working on how to listen to one another more effectively, to try to create understanding as feelings were expressed, and this would not be easy.

"For the next session," I proposed, "I would like to meet with Alice alone, to hear her perspective."

I looked over at her, and she grudgingly nodded. She still wouldn't look at me.

Alice returned a week later, and I was again struck by her reticence and discomfort, looking as if she wanted to shrink into the couch and disappear. In an effort to connect with her and to make her feel more at ease, I asked whether she enjoyed music, and she responded that she did. I mentioned indie music, and she nodded her head, so I began playing Real Estate, Beach House, Au Revoir Simone, and Fleet Foxes, among others.

Alice began to smile. "I haven't heard some of these. Thank you for the introduction." Her resistance began to melt away.

After a while, I asked her, "Would it be alright to ask you a few questions about yourself?"

Following a long silence, she reluctantly agreed. She was deeply mistrustful of me but clearly longed to find a friend to help her out of her messy and profoundly unhappy situation.

"Alice," I said, "when did you begin to feel so upset with your parents? Can you tell me what was going on in your life at that time at home and at school and how you were feeling about it all?"

She began to speak, albeit guardedly and with many pauses.

"Beginning in seventh grade, I started to feel more and more alone at home. There was a lot of pressure at school. I was trying to get accepted into my school's gifted and talented program, and it's really competitive."

Alice also didn't share her father's religious views. "I think I'm at least agnostic and maybe atheist like my mother," she said. "I'm also very curious about Judaism, but I'm afraid to bring any of this up with either of them. My father acts like I'm challenging his authority whenever I question my own beliefs, and he gets angry and cuts off the discussion."

Recalling a comment by my own psychoanalyst some years before, I said to her, "Alice, religious beliefs are very much a personal and private matter. As you continue to grow and develop in your life, only you can decide what parts of each of your parents you will want to bring along with you and what parts of them you will leave behind."

With this comment, I hoped that Alice would begin to feel more comfortable exploring her own identity, instead of feeling scared by her departure from her parents' beliefs.

"I also feel that my parents' rules are excessive, but every time I try to talk to them about it, they get angry and shut me down. It makes me feel like my feelings don't matter, or like they're wrong. This hurts and makes me feel really mad."

I empathized and agreed that it would have been better had she been given a voice, whether her parents agreed with her or not.

"You want them to treat you with respect," I told her, "and to be willing to listen to your point of view, for sure. No wonder you began to feel bad!

"What kind of rules are we talking about?" I asked.

"No computer use on weekday evenings unless it's for a school assignment, weekend curfew of ten o'clock, no texting friends at night, no visiting with my boyfriend at his house even when his parents are at home. There are many others."

As she described the restrictions, she trembled, and I could hear the anger in her voice and see sadness and defiance in her face.

These sounded reasonable for a seventh grader, but unfortunately, they hadn't been eased at all in the past four years. As Alice was speaking, I remembered how badly I had wanted to break the rules laid down by my own parents.

"Alice, as I get to know your parents better and as they, hopefully, begin to trust me and my judgment, you and I will discuss these rules with them and will come to learn the rationale behind the rules, and you can express how you feel. Of course you would like the rules to disappear, and I understand that; but that isn't going to happen. We will work together to develop more trust between you and your parents and to negotiate with them to give you more freedom in return for you demonstrating more responsible behavior. Is this approach acceptable to you?"

She looked a little brighter and a bit hopeful. For the first time, she actually looked up and met my eyes, and she smiled ever so slightly. As the session progressed, she began to open up more. At the third session, I brought her parents back in.

"Alice and I are making some good initial progress," I told them, "but I'd like to see her once a week, and I'd like you two to join us every other week during this crisis period." Eventually, we would reduce their attendance to once a month.

And so Alice and I began to explore her inner world as she began to free associate. Early on, we uncovered that Alice had begun to feel depressed four years earlier, feeling awkward, ugly, less talented than her sister, and never able to please her parents, particularly her father. It wasn't just the rules that got her down, although they were central to her anger; it was more that Alice felt that her parents just didn't know her.

"They've never taken the time to learn who I really am," she said. "They never ask how I feel, and they get angry when I tell them. They don't know me at all."

Their seeming indifference furthered her feelings of worthlessness and undermined the confidence she needed to successfully separate and begin to form an adult identity.

Alice said, "I know I'm a good kid. I've worked hard in school for years, trying to please them, but they always think of me as a bad kid. What's the point of trying to please them anymore?"

She projected onto them many of the negative feelings she had about herself and truly believed that her parents hated her.

And then there was the paradox faced by her parents. To be able to successfully let go of her, they had to get closer to her. They would need to come to understand her hopes, dreams, fears, longings, aspirations, and feelings toward them, by actively engaging with her. They would need to talk with her a lot more often, in a spirit of empathetic listening, if they were ever to trust her enough to make her own decisions. They projected onto Alice many of their own fears and prejudices and stories they had heard about other local teens in trouble rather than really getting to know her.

Alice saw herself as a good kid who wanted to follow rules, just not unreasonable ones. And unlike her sister, Jen, Alice could not blindly obey them without understanding their purpose. She felt terribly disrespected when her parents refused to discuss the reasons for the rules and felt hurt that they believed her to be untrustworthy. This was complicated by the fact that she was struggling to create an identity for herself that was different from her sister's. This made an already challenging developmental task even more so, given that she was a year behind her sister in school and that the two shared a remarkable physical resemblance.

"My teachers and other kids are always comparing me to Jen, like she's some kind of role model. I'm so sick of it!"

I actively empathized with her: "Alice, you are struggling to find yourself, your own path, and an identity that you like and that feels right for you."

It helped to remember what it was like for me at her age—the shouting matches at home, slammed doors, disappearing for hours at a time to find solace in the nearby woods, remembering how much it could hurt being an adolescent and how confusing a time it was.

In our next family session, Randi wept and described her great sadness: "I feel like we've lost our daughter and no longer recognize her!"

I offered Randi some kleenex to dry her tears, and she smiled.

"I'm sorry for crying," she said, "and for using so many tissues!"

Alice's father, Tom, sat sternly and said, "All young men—particularly Eddie—are dogs. They're only interested in sex. They'll seduce multiple girls and then dump them without a second thought. They can't be trusted."

Randi and Tom both believed with all of their hearts that they were protecting Alice from predatory boys with too much testosterone, from a teenage world where rules and boundaries rarely held firm, and from Alice herself, who they perceived as filled with impulses she could barely restrain.

Alice's parents had a much easier time letting go of her older sister. "Jen fully embraces our belief system and rarely challenges the rules. She's so much easier to raise. We feel like we know her better than Alice."

Jen resembled them, so they wouldn't project onto her many of the fantasies they held about Alice, whose defiance and repudiation of many of their rules and beliefs led them to imagine the worst in her. This conflict stoked the fears that led them to control her as opposed to letting go.

To help build a therapeutic relationship with Alice's parents, I identified and empathized with them by saying, "I am also a father of two girls, who are about ten years older than Alice and Jen, and I'm fully aware of what it feels like to live in fear over who your daughter is hanging out with, wondering if she is safe, whether she will return home in one piece and successfully launch herself into college with confidence. The weight of responsibility that you feel for Alice's life is huge, and of course, you only want the best for her. You want to protect her, and at the same time, Alice wants and needs to take on more responsibility and to become more independent. You don't want to live in fear, and, Alice, you don't want to live feeling chronically angry and depressed over your parents' rules. Let's work really hard in the coming months to understand one another and where each of you is coming from." Her parents began to trust me a bit more, and we started to uncover the feelings underlying their rules.

Over the ensuing months, we made slow and steady progress, bringing up the issue of Alice's low self-esteem. We uncovered that, in addition to her depression, she suffered from symptoms of anxiety, at times bordering on panic, which complicated matters. We began to treat this with medication, which helped her feel more in control of at least one area of her life—her mind.

Early on, the sessions were dominated by Alice's relationship with Eddie.

"I should be free to see him as often as I want," she said. "I really care for him."

Her parents wanted her to break off the relationship. "We're worried about changes in Alice's behavior since she began hanging out with him. She has been cutting school with him at lunchtime, and her grades are dropping. And we were shocked and saddened by her giving it up to him. How can we trust her?"

"I empathize with your concerns," I said, "but by arbitrarily establishing rules that you refuse to discuss and by reinforcing them with excessive punishment, you have contributed to Alice feeling hopeless and depressed and to her angrily acting out. I support your responsibility to set the rules, yet at the same time, perhaps the rules could be modified over time, particularly as Alice demonstrates that she can manage increasing levels of responsibility."

We all agreed, after my encouraging Randi and Tom, that it was time to take a risk and let Alice attend a football game to watch Eddie play and then go out to dinner with him. It was time for her parents to lengthen her leash a bit.

"I promise," Alice told me (and I trusted her based on the bond we had formed), "that I'll be home by curfew."

Alice honored her pledge, and this turning point marked a new beginning in her relationship with her parents. They began granting her greater freedom in return for her demonstrating more accountability.

In our individual sessions, Alice and I explored her sadness over how her parents kept Eddie at a distance.

"They never try to get to know him," she said. "He treats me really well. He's nothing like they think."

We explored her envy of her sister, and her sadness and anger over how she felt less loved and disrespected by her parents—and by her sister too. At the end of each individual session, Alice and I would strategize together and create an agenda listing the issues that she wanted to discuss with her parents at the next family session. In thinking through and prioritizing the agenda items and then addressing them with her parents, Alice felt that she had more of a voice and more control over her life. I would alternately empathize with Alice and try to speculate what her parents were thinking and feeling.

"Alice, your parents do love you, and out of that love and a wish to protect you from a teenage world that scares them, they have instituted those rules that you hate so much. Their hearts are in a good place, but their execution leaves something to be desired. You feel hurt by so many of their actions, but perhaps what hurts the most is the feeling that you don't have a voice in your relationship with them and don't feel respected for decisions that you have made, including your choice of Eddie as a boyfriend. It's important that we talk with your parents about all of these issues, if you are willing."

I was walking a fine line, trying to maintain my fragile alliance[1] with Alice, being careful not to side with her or her parents but to empathize, support, and educate. We worked through a great many issues together: what it was like for Alice to be so close in age to her sister and to follow in her footsteps at home and at school, to grow up believing in God and Catholicism and then shifting her beliefs to being an agnostic or atheist or Jewish (she still wasn't sure). We discussed how she both feared and loved her father and felt a deep love for her mother; she had wondered if it was lost forever and then slowly rediscovered it. We questioned whether Eddie would be right for her once she entered college. We discussed that it was okay to be different from her sister, and we developed her exceptional capacity to think about her life and what would bring her happiness.

At the end of a session where Alice had worked really hard to develop some powerful insights into herself and her parents, I said to her, "Alice, you have a remarkable ability to observe yourself and your life in figuring out what is best for you and what is going on inside the minds and hearts of others. You are gifted in this area well beyond your peers. Are you sure you don't want to give up electrical engineering and computer science to pursue a career as a psychotherapist?"

We both laughed, and it felt great to share in her newfound happiness.

Over the eighteen months I spent with Alice and her parents, Randi and Tom got their daughter back, and Alice was able to put her feelings of anger and disappointment into words and to calm her behavior. At one point, she shared (with mild embarrassment) how, "In retrospect, I appreciate that my parents had established and enforced rules. Although I still believe they were too strict, I'm grateful for the lessons they taught me in prioritizing what is important in life. They didn't take the easy way out, as some of my friends' parents have."

Three people who once sat as far apart as possible in my waiting room now snuggled next to one another and joked and laughed together. We began making plans to end the family therapy and move Alice to monthly supportive therapy sessions as she entered college. She had been accepted early decision into an honors computer science program at a respected university, something that had made her parents (and me) immensely proud.

At our farewell family session, I congratulated Alice, Randi, and Tom for all of their hard work and success, and in turn, they thanked me. Inside, I remembered what it was like for our own daughters to leave home and empty out our nest. As I told them that I felt like a proud father myself, now that Alice was successfully launching into her college years, I began to well up with tears, and Alice's mom did as well.

We smiled at each other, and this time around, she reached over to the kleenex box and, with great warmth and gratitude in her eyes said to me, "Now it's my turn to hand these to you."

We hugged one another as we said our goodbyes.

Begin to Heal

For parents, it may be emotionally painful to realize that the baby they once held in their arms is growing up and will soon leave the nest. It raises issues such as aging, recognizing one's mortality, and letting go of some of the hopes and dreams they once held for their child. Alice's story illustrates some important themes regarding these matters. Her separation was complicated by her proximity in age to her sister, which made identity formation more challenging, and by her sister being perceived as "perfect." These themes apply in one way or another to many children who are struggling to separate and individuate and to parents who are striving to do a better job as their children navigate the transition into adulthood.

Use your workbook to write down your answers to the following questions:

Step 1: Examine your own behavior.

Begin by examining yourself and your behavior toward your child. How would you describe your pattern of relating to them? Do you behave in ways that drive them away? If so, how?

Step 2: Avoid excessive criticism.

Do you find yourself frequently criticizing what they are thinking or planning? Write down what specifically triggers your criticism. How might you become less reactive? How might you substitute empathy and curiosity instead? Write down some ideas about how you might react differently to these triggers.

Step 3: Help them determine their own values.

Do you feel the need to impose your ideals or values on them? Which ones do they embrace? Which are repudiated? Which of the values they repudiate concerns you the most? What do you believe will happen to them if they continue down that path?

Step 4: Analyze the reasons for your need to control.

Do you feel out of control and, as a result, take steps to try to control their life? Do you feel frequently frustrated with them? Do you feel helpless and worry that they may be heading over a cliff? Write out specifically why you need to feel more in control. What is your picture of what is going to happen to them? To you? Do others you trust share your point of view or see it differently? How?

Step 5: Manage your anxiety.

Are you driving yourself, your spouse, or your child crazy with your worry and anxiety? Are some of these based in your own neurotic needs? Which ones? Where do you think they originated? Which may constitute an overreaction?

Step 6: Empathize and share with them.

Remember what it was like for you when you passed through this phase of life, and if appropriate, share stories about your own fears and doubts and your successes and setbacks. Which of your tales might you share with them? Please write them down here and evaluate their suitability and likely impact. Help your child understand that it is okay to make mistakes and suffer setbacks; you had plenty of them at their stage of life. This can provide them support and the hope that they will survive them as well.

Step 7: Offer advice—when it's asked for.

Offering unwanted advice serves to undermine your child's confidence in their decision-making. Ask them what they feel they need from you. Let them know that it is okay if they need something different from how you once parented them before. Offer advice if they request it; otherwise, keep it to yourself.

Step 8: Keep talking throughout the transition.

Speak with your child about how you (and they) are going through a major readjustment of roles and responsibilities during this new phase of their life. First, write down your perspectives on what you are going through, then ask about what this phase is like for them. Let them know that you are there to help and that you will take the lead from them on what they need and when they need it. Just as they are trying to figure out who they are and what they want, let them know that you are thinking about how to be the best parent possible at this stage of their life.

Step 9: Communicate with your partner.

It is important to speak frequently with your spouse or partner (and trusted friends) to give and receive support, to commiserate, and to strategize on what interventions (if any) are called for. What agenda items would be included in such a discussion?

Step 10: When necessary, seek professional help.

If your child develops symptoms of excessive anxiety or depression or other worrying signs or you suspect that they may be coping by using drugs or alcohol, then professional help is necessary.

Step 11: Support progressive levels of independence.

Begin trusting your child's judgment, letting them make mistakes. Don't rush to the rescue unless those mistakes threaten to seriously derail their lives. Grant them more freedom as they take on greater responsibility. Establish an atmosphere whereby you gradually and progressively let go, lengthening the leash while trusting them. Recalibrate when they slip up with a nonthreatening conversation about what happened, and apply fair punishments that fit the "crime."

Step 12: Enter their world, thoughtfully.

Inquire about how their life is going. What is happening with their friends? What challenges are they facing at school? How are things going with their girlfriend or boyfriend? Be explicit that you recognize that your child deserves a private life and that you do not wish to intrude. Additionally, be open to listening without passing judgment, and treat their ideas with respect. If you disagree, do so respectfully; your child will be testing and discarding many ideas, and some of them may seem pretty wild.

Step 13: Encourage them to have a voice.

It can be particularly painful when a child who was once loving and caring becomes sullen, angry, and highly critical and disparaging. Try to empathize with the many challenges of separating from home and beginning to form an identity, and remember how that once felt for you. Encourage them to openly express their anger in a respectful way. Explain that you want them to be open and honest about whatever they are feeling in an atmosphere of emotional and physical safety.

Step 14: Be patient.

Be patient and persistent but not annoying or controlling. Don't be afraid to set rules, and discuss the reasons for setting them. Your child may rail against them outwardly yet secretly feel grateful that someone is in charge at a time where they feel so out of control. Give praise when the rules are followed.

Step 15: Encourage them to explore a variety of relationships.

Encourage them to invite their friends over, make their friends feel special and welcomed, and then back away and let them have privacy. The same holds true for their boyfriend or girlfriend. You may not approve of their choice, but keep in mind that it is highly unlikely that this will be the person that they end up marrying. Your child will learn and grow by testing out different relationships with different types of personalities. If your child's behavior begins to deteriorate while they are involved with a friend or romantic interest, don't openly criticize the person they have chosen. Instead, focus on your child's behavior, and discuss with them how it has changed. Where are they going with their behavior? What will it lead to if it continues? What will be the final outcome for them if they continue down that path?

Step 16: Parent cooperatively.

There will be far less strain in your marriage (or with your ex) if each of you gives up preconceived notions of what makes for "good parenting" and you truly listen to one another and work to reach a consensus. There are no perfect parents, and this is a particularly difficult phase in your child's life to successfully navigate. It will likely test the bonds of your relationship with your spouse and will certainly test them with your child. Many times, you may be filled with anxiety and doubt, regardless of what you have read or discussed with other parents.

Step 17: Seek expert help.

If the negative situation with your child remains stuck or progresses downhill, seek out professional help with an expert in treating adolescents, young adults, and their families. Make certain that the therapist includes parents in the treatment process at predictable intervals so that you do not feel completely in the dark as the treatment unfolds. As was the case with Alice, professional help can unstick a troubled developmental process and can place it on a path that leads your child to successfully separate and individuate. It can also help you communicate better with your child and spouse and cope with all of your own life stage issues that may complicate your letting go.

We have been exploring your emotional life and that of your child. In our next session, we will come to understand some of the different types and stages of love relationships and will talk about mature adult love and the development of emotional intimacy. I look forward to talking with you again.

HEAL YOUR
ROMANTIC RELATIONSHIPS

SESSION SEVEN

What Is Mature Love, and How Do I Find It?

Romantic relationships are so important in each of our lives that I would like to spend the next five sessions with you exploring many of the origins of emotional conflict that interfere with them and how these determinants may be identified and untangled in your own life and the lives of those you care about. In the next three sessions, we will cover sources of distress that are common to many intimate relationships. These near-universal themes will be illustrated by the stories of Sharon's individual therapy with me and two of the couples that I treated—John and Mary and Todd and Nancy. We will then devote two sessions to the lingering, mutilating effects of childhood trauma (sexual and physical abuse) on intimate adult relations, which is a special situation that requires professional help, and where you will acquire a deep understanding of the psychotherapy of adult survivors as I share with you the stories of Tara and Brad. In this first session, we will begin by defining mature love and will explore some of the obstacles that arise in our search for an intimate connection.

Perhaps you are searching for love, are newly in love, or are afraid that you or your partner are falling out of love. You believe that love can brighten your life and bring you warmth in a world that is, at best, indifferent and, at worst, cruel. Many of us have experienced that glow at one time or another. At other times, a love relationship may feel very different—like the weight of the world is on your shoulders—the very opposite of something bright and inspiring! How might we better understand these inconsistencies? The questions like this surrounding love are nearly endless: What is the nature of love itself? What are the many manifestations of love? What is "true love"? How do you know if you are really in love? How do you know if your partner genuinely loves you? How do you keep love alive in the face of the inevitable disappointments and hardships of life? What is "mature love"? How do you create a love relationship that is resilient and unwavering?

Television, movies, and romance novels frequently present idealized images of love and relationships that are passionate, blissful, and all encompassing. Unfortunately, our absorption of these pop-culture ideals from a young age all too often leads to unrealistic expectations, which can, in turn, lead to confusion and heartache.[1] To have a successful intimate relationship, we must first understand the constituents of mature love, as opposed to an idyllic fantasy. This is what I hope to illustrate for you in this session.

♪ Session Soundtrack ♪

The song "I Want to Know What Love Is," by Foreigner portrays a lonely man's self-reflection about how love can bring him warmth in a life filled with loneliness as he goes about living in a world that feels cold and indifferent. He wants to know what love is, to end his loneliness, but feels afraid of the heartache and pain that love can bring. Are his fears justified?

Visit DrBruceKehr.com/music-6 for audio files
and further discussion of the soundtracks.

The Three Phases of a Romantic Relationship

In several of our earlier sessions, we talked about emotional development throughout the life cycle and how each phase brings with it new challenges and opportunities to grow and change and how unresolved traumas and conflicts during one phase may resurface to complicate one's life in later phases. The same concepts apply to romantic relationships, which also grow and develop (or stagnate and degenerate into chronic conflicts) throughout their life cycles. Early on, these romantic relationships may pass through three phases, which I've outlined below.

PHASE 1: THE ROMANTICIZED PHASE, OR THE PHASE OF IDEALIZATION

This first phase is where you feel enraptured and incredibly excited about the other person. You are enchanted by them. You are obsessed and think about them almost all of the time. Calls or text messages are frequent, and the other person is the best thing that has ever happened to you. The sex can be amazingly intense and passionate. This phase can last as little as a night or two or as long as several months. However, this romanticized phase will always end. If it ends with a breakup, there are many possible reasons: Perhaps the inevitable disappointments are unacceptable. Perhaps one or both of you are not ready for a real relationship; caring feelings may emerge that feel threatening or frightening. You may begin to see red flags that scream out to you, "Run! Run!" Perhaps your backgrounds, goals, and dreams for the future are just too different. And at times, one or both of you may want to continue to seek out a series of "hot" relationships that renew the excitement of this phase, believing you can eventually find one where these feelings will persist. This phase may also end by transitioning into the "real relationship" of phase 2.

PHASE 2: THE REALITY PHASE

The second phase begins when you are still having fun together and are attracted to each other, but you start to notice each other's flaws. Your partner may let you down or make you angry, or you may feel neglected, poorly treated, or otherwise disappointed. Some of this may be normal disenchantment and is to be expected in a real relationship. At other times, it may be that the person is too self-absorbed to be able to truly satisfy your basic needs (see the "Loving a Narcissist" box on page 133). At the same time, you may develop genuine caring, deeper feelings of affection for one another. Although it may feel a bit scary, you each begin talking about your hopes and dreams for the future—where you would eventually like to settle down, whether you would like to have children, and so on.

The beginning of the reality phase can be difficult to negotiate, and for this reason, many romantic relationships end here. Intimacy and commitment can feel scary and can make you or your partner want to run away, but those feelings can be talked through as opposed to acted on. Previous disappointments in love, significant unresolved losses, parental divorce (or unhappy parents who remain married despite deep conflicts), and growing up in a family characterized by emotional distance can all result in a fear of commitment. Each of these experiences may bring about conscious or unconscious feelings and beliefs that emotional safety in a love relationship is just not possible or sustainable. You may fear that mutual trust, genuine care and understanding, having a voice so that your feelings matter to your partner, being treated with compassion, and deep friendship will never fully materialize or will come about only to later be lost.

At this point, you may be thinking, *This sounds too complicated. Is there anything I can do to prevent phase 2 and stay in the romanticized phase?* Unfortunately, there is no way to avoid the reality phase. But you can work through it with the right person.

You may begin to ask yourself, *Is this person the one?* And if so, *Can I really envision spending the rest of my life with this person? Will our loving feelings deepen and endure or die off?* All of their flaws become more prominent in your mind and your heart. Which ones are acceptable, bearable? Which feel like deal breakers? You may ask yourself, *Will they be willing to give up the deal breakers to make me happy? Will love, respect, and trust endure, or will they eventually betray me by having an affair or leaving? Will they be a good parent? Will some of the differences in our backgrounds complement each other or eventually cause irreparable rifts?*

When you marry someone, you marry into their extended family. What are these people like? Do they make you feel welcome and, eventually, cared about and loved, or are they troubled or emotionally disturbed, critical of you or your partner, distant? Do they make you feel unwanted or excluded? What will be the impact of the family on your life together if you choose to commit? Will they allow you to build a separate life or cross unacceptable boundaries and interfere? These are tough but important questions as you navigate (at times tumultuously) through this phase toward a durable, real relationship.

Because of the inherent vulnerability of opening up intimately to another person and letting them more fully understand you, your flaws, your strengths, and your weaknesses, you may begin to feel really scared. You feel increasingly dependent on them, and your independence feels threatened. You may ask yourself, *How will I be able to remain my own person in this relationship? Will I somehow lose my individuality, aspects of myself that I prize? How will my wish for solitude at times work with our need to be a couple? How will we resolve the conflicts that inevitably arise, and will we have the maturity, commitment, and personal responsibility to see it through?*

There are some big red flags to look for during this phase, any of which will begin to cause emotional strain. For example, frequent disappointments, feeling uncared about, being repeatedly criticized, not feeling accepted for who you are, being told that you are "the problem" (gas lighting), emotional or physical abuse, substance abuse, a lack of a strong work ethic, refusal to take responsibility for their actions, and an unwillingness to listen are but a few examples.

It can be emotionally painful for a relationship to end during this phase. It can elicit feelings of self-doubt, fears that you are not good enough, and concern or regret that things wouldn't have come to an end if you had only behaved differently. Feelings of confusion may arise if you and your partner had seemingly enjoyed your time together both emotionally and physically. Ultimately, if you can each accept the other for who you are—flaws and all—within the context of working on the relationship to bring greater satisfaction, then the bond can develop into a real and durable one—into mature love.

PHASE 3: DURABLE REALITY

The third phase of a romantic relationship is what we might call the **durable reality** phase. Here, you have a wide range of feelings toward that other person. Trust is difficult to establish, fragile, and easily threatened by your own underlying feelings of vulnerability that come from a deepening attachment as emotional intimacy grows. Trust is the bedrock of all durable relationships, and in part, it comes through a growing feeling of emotional safety with your partner. Recognize that each of you feels vulnerable and scared of how dependent you may be growing and that it is important to tolerate these feelings and not act on them, because they will never entirely go away. You may even want to talk with one another about them.[2] At times, you feel love, affection, and sexual excitement. You really enjoy being with them and can't wait to see them. At other times, you may feel furious and want out. You may feel relatively neutral at times and may experience your partner as a companion. At other times, you may feel ambivalent, because your partner can meet some of your needs but not others.

These conflicting feelings are the hallmark of something real. If you work hard to keep the relationship alive and motivate yourself to understand your partner, if you prioritize their happiness along with your own and genuinely try to please them, then it's possible to build a life together of passion, trust, and devotion. This is called **mature love**. To develop and maintain a mature love relationship, it is essential to align your expectations toward what is possible and real, as opposed to what is fantasized and unachievable.

As your love for one another broadens and deepens, a joint commitment to build a life together will (hopefully) emerge. Your lives begin to settle into a series of daily routines, and the excitement of the chase begins to fade away and largely disappear, replaced by a quieter love.

Here is where deeper, largely unconscious vulnerabilities may come into play that were present but not active during the first two phases. As emotional intimacy unfolds and progresses further, previously hidden emotions may unconsciously sabotage[3] the growth and development of a deeper emotional bond. You may hide your true self from the person you love and keep a distance, because it feels too scary to let yourself be all in, to really let yourself go, to feel so vulnerable and dependent. You may hide prior experiences that fill you with shame and humiliation (e.g., a hookup phase before the relationship, having been raped, or having been abused as a child). Sometimes, it may feel that your very identity may be threatened (e.g., "Until recently, I knew myself as an independent woman, fully able to take care of myself. Who is this woman emerging inside of me that feels so dependent on his love, that really needs him? I don't recognize myself anymore!"). There are many reasons for distancing behaviors in relationships, including disturbances in the types of attachment that we form in childhood.[4]

In mature love, there is mutual respect, a willingness to listen and to understand, even when you vehemently disagree. The other person becomes the number-one priority in your life. You try to give one another emotional support, compassion, and empathy during difficult times (life is hard on everyone; it is just harder on some folks than on others). Their happiness in life becomes paramount, and you are their greatest cheerleader. You try to talk about anything and everything as friends. Every day, you try to display small acts of affection (e.g., when buying groceries, bringing home their favorite berries or a special treat that will make them smile). You learn how to resolve the inevitable bumps in the road by authentically and openly talking them through, listening to one another, and generating options to arrive at a compromise.

At times, even a satisfying, mature love relationship can fall into a crisis, manifested by stagnation or continuing conflict. Prior repressed and unresolved emotional traumas, upsetting life events, and aging and health concerns can all serve to undermine what had been very satisfying. Here, again, self-reflection and analysis and individual or couples therapy can make a significant difference in bringing about understanding that will unstick the relationship, provide a tangible pathway toward improvement, and restore the prior feelings of satisfaction and an intimate bond.

Sharon's Story

Sharon was twenty-eight years old and feeling confused, lost, and despondent about her prospects for finding a man to love and marry. In her early twenties, when she lived in New York City, she had led a somewhat wild life, with frequent partying, unprotected sex with a fair number of partners, and experimentation with marijuana and cocaine. As the manager of one of the hottest clubs in Manhattan's meatpacking district, she was able to wield power by determining who got to bypass the long lines out front and who was awarded the best seats in the house, and she was sought after by a number of local rock bands who coveted being engaged to play at the club. Their male lead singers would frequently come on to Sharon, and at the time, it made her feel highly sexually desired, although she eventually tired of their self-absorption and efforts to manipulate her. Eventually, still single, she relocated to the DC area to be near her siblings.

Sharon was the ultimate fashionista, and that was one of the attributes that first attracted Elliott to her. He was young but already highly successful as a private equity fund executive. Elliott was extremely good looking, wore expensive clothes, and used to pick Sharon up in his Porsche and take her to the finest restaurants in Washington. She dated him for over a year, fell in love, and wanted to marry him. Although the sex was terrific, she nonetheless felt a kind of emptiness when she was with him. He was highly self-absorbed, always talked about himself, and rarely asked how she was doing or even what she was thinking or feeling. The relationship was exciting but unfulfilling.

In our first session, as she was describing her relationship with Elliott, I asked, "Sharon, how do you really feel when you are with him?"

To her surprise, she recalled that she had never been very happy.

"I haven't actually thought about this much . . . but he tends to put me down and find flaws in me. This makes me angry and sad, but I don't think I've ever told him so. He's never really gotten to know me as a person."

"Do you have any thoughts on why you've stayed with him for so long despite your unhappiness?"

Sharon didn't have an answer to my question, and so I suggested that she begin to give me a history of her childhood and young adulthood and that the answer might emerge from her story.

Somewhat reluctantly, Sharon began to share her upbringing. "I was raised in an upper-middle-class family near Chicago, where my father practiced law. I knew that he loved me, but we were never emotionally close; he was either focused on his work or doting on my mother. My mother is petite and extraordinarily beautiful. She often criticizes me, especially my appearance—saying that my nose is too large, that I'm too heavy, that I'm dull and stupid. My father just stands by, helpless. She'd often say, 'If only you looked more like me.' That probably wasn't great for my self-image."

Sharon's mother always wore designer clothes and accessories, even when she was out running errands. She was so obsessed with her own image and beauty and so absorbed in shopping sprees with her girlfriends that she would often forget to pick Sharon and her two sisters up at play dates or school functions.

"This was embarrassing. My friends' mothers would be forced to take me home, sometimes complaining about my mother's unreliability."

As I listened, I recalled my own mother's unreliability and how it had made me feel. Using my countertransference reaction, I said, "Sharon, you may have felt humiliated when those other mothers commented on your mother's undependability. It would also be understandable if you felt sad and abandoned by her. As a young girl, did you feel that your mother's neglect resulted from something being wrong with you?"

With that, she burst into tears. "Yes!" she said. "My mother would get mad at me when I would ask what happened. She would say, 'Mind your own business, Sharon!' I'd feel crushed, unworthy of love, abandoned, and insignificant. It was like I was an afterthought in her life. Or worse still, I'd sometimes feel so unwanted, that I never should have been born."

I handed her some kleenex as she sobbed, and I felt bad for her. At that moment, I could envision a sweet little girl inside of her—one who felt alone.

"Sharon, you didn't deserve to be treated that way. Your mother was neglectful and then wouldn't take responsibility for her negligence. You describe her as incredibly self-absorbed. Her behavior had nothing whatsoever to do with you or how lovable or desirable you were."

Trying to give her some hope at a really low moment, I said, "Sharon, you impress me as someone with a great deal of love to give, and you possess so many strengths. You have a beauty inside of you that you may have locked away many years ago, behind all of this sadness and anger you feel. That optimistic little girl is still inside you, ready to find love and affection, and I just know you will."

On her face was the faint hint of a hopeful smile.

As we continued our work together, Sharon began to realize that her deep feelings of being unlovable, like she was damaged goods, were largely the result of her mother's inability to love anyone. She came to recognize that her father loved her, recalling moments of special tenderness with him.

"I realize that he had probably felt trapped in a loveless marriage but had remained to provide some comfort and guidance to me and my sisters. At the same time, I'm angry with him for not leaving my mother and taking us along. He should have protected me from my mother. He should have reined in her spending habits, which forced him to work long hours and frequently travel to other cities. This took him even further from me and my sisters and left us even more exposed to my mother's cruelty."

I said, "It sounds like you felt loved by your father in certain ways, but not in some of the important ways that you yearned for. You felt sad and angry that he didn't protect you more from your mother's neglect and devastating criticism. Perhaps you longed at times to tell him how much you needed him to comfort you—to nurture, care for, and protect you."

Sharon began to sob again, and a flood of memories and feelings began to come back related to some of the origins of her self-loathing. In this phase of her therapy, Sharon began to **abreact**,[5] a highly important aspect of treatment that would help her to heal and become whole.

There were many sessions when Sharon openly wept over how deeply her mother had hurt her and where she angrily railed against her mother's criticism and father's passivity and weakness. Over time, she was able to grieve the childhood she longed for but never had and was able to put her parents into perspective and recognize how their personal difficulties affected how they had treated her. The process involved Sharon recollecting, with intense feelings, many painful interactions with her parents that she had internalized[6] as examples of how she was defective and unlovable.

As we examined each of these events through adult eyes, Sharon learned how to separate herself and her self-perceptions from parents whose personal problems had led them to behave in ways that damaged her self-esteem. This process enabled Sharon to develop a more realistic understanding of herself and her parents and helped her let go of those distorted self-perceptions. She learned that she was worthy of being loved and began to love herself.

While we were working together to untangle her heart, Sharon met Matt and began to fall in love, although not in the way she had dreamed.

"With Elliott," who she still saw from time to time, "it's hot and intense for an evening or two, then he disappears for a week or more. He's ostensibly on a road trip for business. He claims he's in meetings that go late into the evening, so he can't call me. I'm not sure that I believe his explanations anymore."

She never felt that he was developing an attachment to her and believed that he would probably never fully commit. She had heard from her girlfriends that Elliott was a player who prided himself in sleeping with multiple women at a time, but Sharon had initially refused to believe them.

"With Matt, it's different," she said, "—a quieter love. He has been more attentive from the beginning and calls almost daily just to see how my day is going. He's not flashy, drives a Honda sedan, and is an executive at a defense contractor. He dresses okay and likes to show me a good time, but he has none of Elliott's pizazz. Nothing about Matt is flashy, but he's devoted, caring . . . and he seems genuinely interested in getting to know me."

Matt was a thoughtful and caring lover, but Sharon would sometimes fantasize about being with Elliott when she was making love to Matt. This would make her feel guilty, but she became deeply attached to Matt, and the two of them began to talk about building a life together. Eventually, she broke things off completely with Elliott.

Sharon and Matt became engaged and then married, and she gave birth to two girls. For the first time in her life, Sharon began to feel loved and lovable, but she still longed at times for the life she had when she was younger, filled with drama and excitement—and Elliott.

"I sometimes think about what life would be like if I'd married him instead," she said. "We'd have a big house, expensive cars, a nanny, and travel to exotic places." Wistfully, she commented, "I have none of that with Matt."

We came to understand that, in her imagined life with Elliott, she could be like her mother in certain ways—wearing premium brands; living a flashy, affluent lifestyle with the freedom to not work and to go shopping with her friends; becoming the diva married to a wealthy man.

At these times, Sharon felt depressed about her life with Matt.

However, she came to realize that the life she imagined with Elliott was just a fantasy. She recalled that he had never been faithful or able to commit and that, although their weekends were filled with expensive and glamorous outings, she had never felt an emotional connection with him. She imagined that Elliott desired and loved her, but he never expressed those feelings in reality.

In one of our sessions, I pointed out, "In some respects, your relationship with Elliott was a repetition of some of the dynamics in your parents' marriage. With Elliott, you assumed your father's role of being in love with a highly attractive narcissist, yet, just like your father did with your mother, you frequently felt helpless with Elliott. He did whatever he wanted, and your job was to tag along and be supportive—all the while without much of an emotional connection. Elliott was a lot like your mom—glamorous, cold, and self-absorbed. Unconsciously, you believed that if you could some-how please Elliott and get him to love you, it would be equivalent to your narcissistic mother finally loving you. Doesn't this behavior of yours also sound a lot like how your father related to your mother: constantly trying to please her but always coming up short as she never felt satisfied or genuinely loved him?"

She thought about this for a minute and agreed. "I'm surprised by how much I've become just like my father. Maybe it's a way of feeling closer to him. After all, he's the only one who ever loved me when I was a child."

Over time, as Sharon was able to accept the reality of Elliott's narcissistic personality, the power of her fantasies began to fade, and she was able to enjoy her young children and Matt's devotion to them and to her. It was a quieter, fuller life—one in which she felt loved and valued just for being herself.

Initially, Sharon's idealization of her relationship with Elliott interfered with her developing emotional intimacy with Matt. In the course of our work together, she came to understand that her fantasies about a glamorous life with Elliott were a kind of unconscious antidote to the self-loathing that she had developed as a child, to the anger she felt toward her mother, and to the other sources of low self-esteem. Sharon ultimately accepted that it was an empty fantasy; no amount of money can compensate for the absence of love.

Loving a Narcissist

Like Sharon, many adults repeatedly become engaged with narcissistic personalities.[7] Due to unconscious forces, a lack of self-esteem, repetition of earlier formative relationships, and a compulsion to repeat self-sabotaging behaviors, they seek out love relationships (and enter business relationships) that are destined from the beginning to bring heartache and failure. What makes them repeatedly tangle up their lives in this way?

To answer this question, we are reminded of that famous quote from Aristotle: "Knowing yourself is the beginning of all wisdom." Many patients first come in for psychotherapy in the middle of a crisis, when they recognize a pattern of failed relationships, or feel chronically unhappy. We learn in the course of therapy that they repeatedly choose narcissists as lovers and companions. We also uncover the sources of their low self-esteem that serve to perpetuate this pattern (e.g., the relationships between one's parents and even grandparents). Through the process of therapy, they can make healthier choices—seeking out partners who provide mature and durable love, an emotional connection, and support and empathy. Successful therapy helps to ensure that future relationships do not wither away and die but remain alive and vibrant.

One of the hallmarks of a narcissistic personality is excessive self-absorption. The narcissist is rarely, if ever, truly interested in others. They may go on at length about themselves but rarely demonstrate a meaningful interest in you. They may feign interest to get you into bed or manipulate you

continued on next page

in other ways to seemingly gratify your needs, but they never truly attempt to form a deeper understanding of you as a person. They are dedicated to meeting their own needs.

Narcissists are incapable of true empathy. They may be able to fake it, because they are intelligent enough to have learned the concept of empathy and may use it as a technique to manipulate others and win people over. (As one of my patients with a narcissistic personality disorder once put it, "I know what empathy is and what to say to sound empathetic but have never felt it.")

True empathy requires compassion and understanding—capacities that the narcissist profoundly lacks. When they attempt empathy, it has a shallow quality that will not resonate within you emotionally and that will lack an authentic emotional connection. Genuine empathy is felt as a deep emotional resonance within your heart that comes along with a caring emotional connection with another human being.

The narcissist is only interested in their own happiness. In their world, you exist only to make them happy. A narcissist attends to your happiness only when it can bring them something they desire or covet—whether that is showing you off to others, getting you into bed, or manipulating some favor out of you. It is all about boosting their self-esteem and sense of self by fulfilling their own needs. In contrast, someone capable of mature love is concerned about their own happiness but is also genuinely committed to helping you find happiness in your own life.

Another core attribute of many narcissists is infidelity. They may engage in one or more affairs—at times, with someone close to them and their lover, thereby not only betraying their lover but also enabling a friend to betray the lover as well. The narcissist may be extremely attractive, charming, interesting, fun, and exciting in the early phases of a relationship. They may sweet-talk you—saying how important you are to them and how much they need you in their life. However, the narcissist can talk the talk, but they cannot walk the walk.

Eventually, the narcissist will show you their true colors. Count on them to betray you—to bolt when reality, ambivalence, or conflict that doesn't resolve in their favor starts to enter the relationship. This abandonment may be at an emotional level, where they withdraw from you into excessive self-absorption (this is not the same as needing some solitude from time to time), or they may end the relationship to move on to the next object of their narcissistic desire. When the inevitable conflicts arise in a real relationship, count on the narcissist to focus on your flaws and the various ways you don't satisfy them, as opposed to working toward an understanding of your needs and point of view.

The narcissist can outwardly radiate a great aura of confidence and competence that may be beguiling. At times, this may be expressed as arrogance. This posturing often masks deep feelings of insecurity, inadequacy, and unmet dependency that are threatening and frightening to them at an unconscious level. The narcissist may jealously and possessively attempt to control you or may, alternatively, distance themselves emotionally, all of which threaten the development of true intimacy. Therefore, a relationship with a narcissist can feel like a very lonely place, even when you're together and participating in an active social life.

Therapy can be a place of hope for narcissistic personalities and their partners, as long as the narcissist is willing to learn, grow, and change. Like each of us, they have had their share of emotional pain, and many can engage in a therapeutic relationship to discover and recover from the early relationships in their own life that led to their personality style. They may initially view therapy as a narcissistic injury, a wound to their pride, and will resist the idea. Remind them that the therapist is not going to blame them for the problems: Rather, they will, in a nonjudgmental fashion, help the two of you to explore how and why the relationship went off track and will begin to create more understanding.

Begin to Heal

Perhaps you or someone close to you can relate to Sharon's story. The self-sabotaging pattern is one whereby love relationships are broken off when the idealization phase ends. A difficult time in a love relationship may cause you or your partner to long for romance with another or actually cheat. Disillusionment is inevitable in all romantic relationships, so let's try to explore yours to see if you can make it more satisfying.

Use your workbook to reconstruct your love relationship by writing down your answers to the following questions. At the end of this exercise, you can use what you learn to sit down with your partner and begin to untangle your hearts together.

Step 1: Start with a description of your partner.

How would you describe the one you love? Please list as many attributes—both positive and negative—as possible.

Step 2: Describe your connection.

Describe in detail the history of your emotional relationship with them. Has there been an emotional connection? A void? Both? Have you felt basically loved over time? Think about your relationships with your closest guy or girlfriends—is your partner able to be there for you in similar ways? Write out the similarities and differences. During times when you have been in emotional pain, have they been there for you? Describe how they behaved at these times.

Step 3: Describe what led to the problems.

When did the relationship go off track and what was happening at the time in your life? In your partner's life? What were you and your partner dealing with in your personal or work lives that may have caused one of you to withdraw, or act in a cruel fashion toward the other?

Did you then enter a cycle of mutual hurt and misunderstanding? What was said and done to hurt one another? Although you may no longer feel in love, your love for your partner may be buried under feelings that arose from those repeated misunderstandings, such as disappointment, sadness, anger, humiliation, and other conscious and unconscious feelings. Please recall when you last loved your partner, and then write out the events that transpired that damaged your loving feelings and how these events made you feel.

Step 4: Describe the history of your relationship.

Write out a history of your relationship together and summarize both the good and satisfying times and the emotionally painful and hurtful times. As you write, be honest about what you specifically did or didn't do to help or hurt the relationship. Did you try to resolve conflicts or simply want your way? Were you willing to compromise? Also write down what your partner did that made you feel abandoned, hurt, and angry.

Step 5: Compare your versions of history.

Once you have created a detailed reconstruction of what happened from your perspective, ask your partner if they would be willing to sit down with you to go over it, in the spirit of presenting what you have written and listening to their perspective. Frame the discussion as an effort to end the cycle of unhappiness for both of you by creating an understanding of what went wrong and how it can be improved.

Step 6: Apologize.

It often helps to begin with an apology for ways that you behaved that were mean, hurtful, or indifferent. Note the specifics of what you were going through at the time, and emphasize that you hadn't meant to hurt your lover, but you were in so much pain yourself that you weren't aware of your insensitive behavior. Write out your apology here.

Step 7: Focus on the positive.

Try to focus on the good aspects of your partner. One way to do this is to make up a "gratitude list"—attributes you are grateful for in them. Add one item to the list each day. Start by listing five of those attributes here, and share the list with your partner. Ask them if they would be willing to create a similar list of what they feel grateful for in you.

Step 8: (Re)develop mutual respect.

Treat each other with respect, even at times where feelings of love are absent. This is another key ingredient. How could you behave more respectfully? List the ways.

Step 9: Work together.

They will never be able to satisfy and gratify all of your desires and longings, but, like Sharon, you can work with your partner to create a durable love relationship where you both feel loved and valued.

What might you work on in yourself to make them feel happier? What are you willing to commit to?

Step 10: Honestly assess your emotional maturity.

You or your partner may simply be incapable of mature love at this time. There could be multiple reasons for this: Perhaps the timing isn't right, or one or both of you fear intimacy, are excessively emotionally dependent, push too hard to move forward, hold back emotionally or physically, or harbor excessive and unresolved narcissism. Perhaps one of you is suffering from an identity crisis. Reflect on any earlier dysfunctional or traumatic love relations. In addition to writing these down in your workbook, it may help to engage in this process of introspection with a trusted friend or in psychotherapy.

* * *

Here's the bottom line: If your relationship is in trouble, work toward developing a strong foundation within yourself and then insist on some fundamental changes in the relationship, or move on. The loneliest place in the world can be a marriage or other long-term relationship where the potential for emotional intimacy is ever present, but it is never realized. Your fear of being alone is real, but ending the relationship will offer the opportunity to find love with someone else—someone who can truly love you!

If you try these steps and they don't work, seek out a couples therapist. If your partner is unwilling to go with you, seek individual therapy in which the therapist can help you develop a strategy and tactics to engage your lover in a dialogue around these issues to get them to commit to entering therapy with you. If you continue to feel miserable in the relationship and your partner refuses all conversation and help, get the emotional support you need from your therapist, friends, and family to leave. You deserve to be in a relationship characterized by mature adult love. Don't settle for anything less.

SESSION EIGHT

What Makes Commitment So Challenging?

In the previous session, we determined what makes a mature (as opposed to narcissistic) romantic relationship and what the pitfalls of maintaining that relationship may be. In this session, I aim to dive deeper into the most mature commitments we will ever enter into: marriage and other long-term committed relationships. Marriage is one of the most challenging of all human relationships. It can also be one of the most emotionally rewarding. True intimacy—including friendship, compassion, empathy, sharing and realizing dreams together, advising, comforting and supporting each other through life, sexual satisfaction, and deep love and affection—is attainable, but it can feel far out of reach. Feeling emotionally safe with one another may come and go. Marriage and other long-term committed relationships are characterized by highs and lows—times of joy and times of despair, tender intimate moments and periods fraught with conflict and emotional distance.

Your wedding is typically a time of joy, love, and tender feelings toward one another. What happens to these feelings over time? What makes any intimate romantic bond so complicated? To begin with, we need to understand what tangles up our human hearts when we engage in deeply intimate human relationships.

Emotional and sexual intimacy stir up deeply felt and largely unconscious[1] conflicts, feelings, and fantasies. Dependence and independence, loyalty and betrayal, satisfaction and disappointment, commitment and fear of abandonment, trust and mistrust, narcissistic love and mature love, freedom and self-sacrifice are just some of the conflicting emotions that characterize any romantic bond and are most intensely experienced in a marriage or other committed long-term relationship. These conflicts, if they remain unconscious and unresolved, can damage a relationship and create emotional distance.

In addition, our early emotional experiences with our mothers and fathers become significant determinants of how all of these unconscious emotional issues are played out in later intimate relations. Disappointments in the love affairs of adolescence and young adulthood also shape our feelings and expectations in adult relationships, as can a prior separation or divorce. Biological, social or environmental, life stage, and existential issues can also come into play. If your spouse has ADHD, depression, anxiety, or a substance abuse problem, additional burdens are placed on what is already a complex relationship. Despite these complications, many of us feel internal and external pressure to get married and then to remain committed to the marriage. Social convention, the values we are taught, and "encouragement" by family members may all add to one's sense of burden.

♪ **Session Soundtrack** ♪

Carly Simon's "The Way I've Always Heard It Would Be" expresses the sadness felt by an adult child over the state of her parents' marriage, portraying a scene where her mother and father are emotionally estranged from one another. As a result, she no longer dreams her sweet dreams. Without question, our childhood experiences of our parents' marriage (or separation and divorce) shape our emotional outlook toward our own marriage. If we are unmarried, they shape how we feel about the prospect of getting married and how that marriage will go or how we may come to feel in any long-term love relationship.

These feelings are poignantly portrayed in Lou Rawls' "Love is a Hurtin' Thing." For every thrill, there is another heartache, happiness gives way to loneliness, and love can bring so much joy and pain, too. He laments that love's road is rough, and the going gets tough.

Visit DrBruceKehr.com/music-7 for audio files and
further discussion of the soundtracks.

Not uncommonly, when a couple comes in to see me for therapy, there is an atmosphere of crisis and fear that the relationship is over. Their life together feels like a tangled mess. What happened? Not uncommonly, the intimate bonds have been severely damaged, but the couple did not become aware of this until long afterward. The pressures of dual careers, raising children, and finances often result in what was once the most special relationship being relegated to second, third, or fourth place in the hierarchy of what is attended to, cared for, and nurtured. This neglect, along with one or more unrecognized and unspoken major disappointments and emotional wounds, derails what had once been a stable and mutually satisfying union.

Gradually, the special bond deteriorates and may be replaced by hostility, indifference, and escalating conflict, at times in front of the children. This can lead to tearful nights, angry dawns, mutual feelings of hatred, and repeated wounds to one another.

They may no longer feel in love with their partner, yet these loving feelings may still exist, buried under conscious and unconscious feelings of anger, sadness, disappointment, and humiliation. The opposite of love is not hate; it is indifference. And feeling hatred toward your partner does not mean the relationship is dead.

One or both partners may hold a negative, dark view of marriage or any long-term committed relationship, but it doesn't have to be this way. If you and your partner remain stuck in an uncomfortable place, it may be difficult to untangle without assistance from a couples therapist. At the outset, the goal of therapy is neither to save nor to civilly end the relationship. There *is* no preconceived agenda, other than creating a safe and open environment to begin to explore what happened to what was once a highly satisfying bond. It will help you determine where it went off track. Not uncommonly, deep misunderstandings developed, and mutual hurtful actions served to usher in a downward spiral in your emotional relations. Once the initial causes are identified, talked through, and understood, forgiveness and empathy can begin to develop. Neurobiological factors can be addressed by medication management and individual therapy. Earlier shared passions can be rediscovered as a result of the initial healing, which, in turn, can transform that downward spiral into a more hopeful future.

It is not inevitable that you will lose yourself in an intimate romantic relationship. It is highly possible to maintain and even strengthen your identity and self while deepening the bonds of attachment and love between you and your partner. If the two of you can prioritize one another's independence, as opposed to behaving in a jealous and possessive fashion, your love can grow even stronger. Place a priority on your partner's freedom to preserve their sense of independence. (That could be as simple as encouraging them to have a regular boys' or girls' night out or continuing their pursuit of a solo hobby they loved before they loved you.) Refrain from attempting to control or dominate your partner. How would you feel if they did that to you?

This doesn't mean that you can't express your preferences or let them know when they do something upsetting. It doesn't mean total acceptance of everything they say or do. In an emotionally healthy relationship, each of you must have a voice and must feel safe to express it. It also means picking your battles, not commenting on every behavior or idiosyncrasy that you find disappointing or irritating. Treating each other with respect, even when your love feels absent, is another key ingredient.

Noted journalist and author Mignon McLaughlin once said that "a successful marriage requires falling in love many times, always with the same person." The implication here is that one can fall in *and* out of love many times in a long-term committed relationship. Many couples who come to me for treatment are convinced that they have fallen out of love and despair over ever rediscovering those feelings with one another. They feel angry, even enraged at their partner, and underneath that anger (which can be a kind of smokescreen) are many other feelings, such as pain, disappointment, sadness, abandonment, fear, anxiety, mistrust, shame, and humiliation.

In the process of working on the relationship and working through these feelings, couples become surprised that seemingly dead loving feelings begin to resurface. Your feelings are not dead; they are submerged under the weight of a series of damaging experiences with one another, primarily driven by misunderstanding and mutual wounds that have eroded the once-strong bonds of love.

At times, the couple may attend to the relationship too late in this cycle of destruction, and the foundation of love has been shattered. However, if a couple has the courage to face up to and work through their feelings, they can rediscover their love and begin to delight once again in each other's company.

The Power of Listening to Your Partner with Curiosity and Empathy

Listening has an enormously powerful effect when a loving relationship has been damaged. When you feel hurt and angry with your partner, listening may be the last thing on your mind. You may want to lash out angrily or retreat. These feelings are understandable, but they perpetuate the emotional damage and a cycle of repeated hurts and recriminations. You may feel emotionally unsafe and untrusting and may want to create distance. To break this cycle, you should adopt a style best characterized as **curious and empathetic** and should even learn how to assist your loved one in figuring out what is going on inside of them. Here are some ideas to help you understand and implement these principles in more detail. Don't be afraid to be the first one to try this method, even if you have been holding out due to wounded pride.

Listen from Your Heart

The most effective type of listening is best characterized as empathetic and compassionate. Pay attention without interrupting. Take note of what your partner says, and really try to understand what you are being told, even if you vehemently disagree with it. Put yourself in your partner's place and work hard to understand what they have experienced. Listen with a spirit of curiosity and cooperation, of jointly embarking on a journey of discovery, even when it is emotionally painful. Convey your understanding without hostility, and, whenever possible and where it is true, take responsibility for your own destructive or neglectful behavior. These are the core elements of developing emotional safety in the relationship, a powerful and necessary step in achieving deep emotional intimacy.

Be Willing to Take the First Step

Alter your own behavior; hopefully, this will encourage your partner to follow suit. End the negative downward spiral where each of you refuses to budge. Become curious about what is going on inside your partner: What is in their heart and on their mind? What are they feeling and thinking about?

Empathetic, Thoughtful, and Respectful Listening Creates a Feeling of Safety

A readiness to blame your partner is the surest way to reinforce feelings of vulnerability and rejection and to discourage the honest sharing that is needed. How often in our lives do we feel listened to and understood by those we care about? If you are honest with yourself, the answer most likely is "not very often" or even "never."

True Listening Restores a Positive Emotional Connection

The healing power of empathetic and compassionate listening should never be underestimated. By injecting a needed dose of hope into the relationship, it enables your partner to feel special and loved. True listening helps to restore a caring emotional connection and positive momentum, particularly when it is followed up by behavior that is more giving and loving and that demonstrates that you have heard what was said and are willing to honor and respect it through purposeful, responsive action.

John and Mary's Story

John and Mary had been married for fifteen years when they came for therapy. They were in the middle of a marital crisis that had begun when Mary discovered that John was having an online affair with a woman named Cindy. John had attended grad school with Cindy years before, and he had received a friend request from her on Facebook. Initially, their correspondence was platonic and innocent enough. Over time, they introduced sexually provocative language, with Cindy sharing revealing pictures of herself, suggesting that she and John should get together so he could sample some of what she was showing him.

Mary had eventually noticed that John was acting differently. One evening, John had left his computer unlocked, and Mary began to look through his emails, where she discovered the online romance. She confronted him, they got into a huge argument, and, in the aftermath, they made an appointment to see me.

This was a second marriage for both of them. At the time of their first visit, Mary was a network security engineer for a private computer services company that customized cybersecurity applications for large database installations. She had been granted a Top Secret government clearance, affording her access to highly sensitive data that affected national security. In her prior marriage, she had had two daughters, now in their mid- and late twenties. Her first husband was an alcoholic, prone to outbursts of rage, who had struck her on several occasions and who had terrified their young children. Mary decided to leave him to save her own life and to try to create a more peaceful and stable home life for her daughters.

About a year later, she met John, who was a quiet, thoughtful, somewhat introverted man with a PhD in aerospace engineering who was currently working for NASA. John had been briefly married to his high-school sweetheart, Karen, when they were in college. He had divorced her, longing for an independent adult life and feeling that Karen was too clingy and needy for him to ever feel independent within the marriage.

John was in his midthirties when he met Mary. He quickly fell in love with her passionate, outgoing, fun-loving personality, blonde hair, and voluptuous figure. She fell in love with his quiet, calm demeanor, the lack of drama in their relationship, and his even-tempered approach to life and love.

"He treated me like a lady," she said—something she had deeply longed for in her first marriage. She also loved his keen intellect, his focus on physical fitness, and his rugged good looks. John reminded Mary of the Marlboro Man. It was a classic example of opposites attract. They had a relatively brief courtship, characterized by intense physical passion, and were soon married.

There were significant initial challenges to their relationship: "John's parents hated me," Mary said. "They couldn't stand the fact that I was a divorcée with two young children and believed their son could do much better."

"My father was also somewhat like Mary's first husband," John added. "He was prone to drinking too much and to angry outbursts of criticism. And my mother drank to excess herself but just passively sat back and watched him tear us apart."

Mary had been estranged from her own parents and siblings for several years. In turn, John felt that Mary's children were cold and unaccepting of him.

"I think they blame me for her divorce," he said.

Adding to the stress was the fact that Mary's first husband increasingly began to distance himself from their children, which seemed to worsen their angry feelings toward John.

John and Mary's relationship had been severely damaged over the years as a result of these issues. Our work was cut out for us. I began thinking about how fortunate I'd been to have loving in-laws and the enormous strain it can place on a love relationship when your spouse never feels embraced by your parents. As a result, I commented to both Mary and John (in part to begin to build a therapeutic relationship and in part to model empathy and compassion), "As you describe life with your extended families once you became a couple, right from the beginning, they treated you shabbily, which probably put both of you under significant emotional strain. These experiences can reduce the odds of survival for any new relationship. Each of you may have felt criticized, judged, and even abandoned by them when you wanted to share with them the joy of your newfound love. But they repudiated you in a really hurtful way. Some couples' love would not have withstood these conditions, but it is clear that your love for one another has endured in spite of this onslaught of negative feelings and behaviors.

"My grandmother used to say, 'If it's meant to be, it's meant to be.' It is clear that you two are meant to be. You love each other very much in spite of this crisis. That is a real strength that we will build on as we work together to help each of you understand how your relationship got to this distressing state and how we can help the two of you move forward to greater satisfaction."

We met for therapy on a weekly basis over about four months, and John was seen by a colleague in individual therapy and received antidepressant medication as well. Their story unfolded as follows.

Their initial love for one another had remained strong and endured multiple family moves while John pursued his PhD and took a series of positions in different states.

"Our immediate family life may have not been the warmest or closest," John said, "but it was vastly preferable to her estranged family and my critical, alcoholic father and passive mother."

Mary added, "For fifteen years or so, we had the typical ups and downs of any married couple, and our lives kept moving on relatively unscathed."

As John and Mary recounted the tale of their families, I felt sadness, anger, and disappointment related to my own family of origin, which bore a number of similarities to theirs. This countertransference reaction helped me to empathize with them and develop an initial strategy for therapy.

"Mary and John," I said, "your estrangement from your families of origin may well fill you with feelings of sadness and longing and a need to grieve what will never be possible with them. And yet it brings you the opportunity to find love in your nuclear family, to make it far more loving and satisfying. This may be a yearning inside each of you. If you like, this is an area where we could focus our work, to make your relationships with each other and with your children as rewarding as possible." They liked this idea.

We began to talk about how both Mary and John had longed for love from their parents and siblings. Each then talked about how their family members had treated them with hostility, judgment, narcissism, and emotional distance. This led to Mary and John each beginning to grieve the family they longed for but never had. In giving up on the possibility of love from members of their extended family, over time, John and Mary were able to begin to focus instead on the abundant love of their nuclear family.

In the months preceding John's cyber affair, several traumatic events occurred. John's father had a fatal accident while driving drunk. A month later, his mother accidentally set herself on fire by falling asleep while smoking a cigarette. She was not badly burned but developed panic attacks and depression and began calling John every day to voice her complaints and fears.

In the middle of these traumas, Mary left John for a month to provide onsite cybersecurity services for a prestigious client in a distant state.

"She'd be so excited when she called," John said. "She'd passionately relate how important her team's work was for maintaining our national security. But I was home alone, feeling worse and worse about my parents. In retrospect, I had begun feeling lonely, desperate, and depressed."

In the grips of his despair and Mary's absence, he began to strike up the relationship with Cindy.

During their treatment, we reconstructed how their love relationship went off the tracks. I encouraged each of them to listen and try to understand one another's feelings, to develop a curiosity about what had been going on inside the other, and to try to empathize with (while not necessarily agreeing with) the feelings that emerged. This style, with your therapist's assistance exploring and clarifying events, feelings, and patterns of behavior, can begin to facilitate the healing process.

I have observed a common pattern over the years. At the beginning of a love relationship, each partner regards the other as the most important person in their life. And then they put so much energy into their careers and family that the love begins to wither and sometimes dies. In Mary and John's case, his love for her began to fade when he felt unwelcome and estranged from her children and when he felt that she favored them over him. Mary began to explore her own reasons why, in retrospect, she didn't continue to give John first place in her heart.

"I felt guilty about breaking up my marriage with the father of my children," Mary said. "I'm worried that I emotionally scarred my kids. I realize now that this led me to overindulge them—at John's expense. I overlooked their unwillingness to embrace him into the family."

Her revelation helped John understand that Mary's intentions were not to hurt or neglect him but, rather, to protect her daughters from further emotional harm. With this perspective, he was able to take it less personally.

We then moved on to his relationship with his parents and his father's alcoholism and related death.

"I'm sorry, John," Mary said. "I could have been more supportive during your crisis over your father's accident. I never should have left your side. I should have been there for you."

"It's okay," John responded. "You actually offered to not be present at the client site, to remain behind to support me, but I encouraged you to go."

They jointly spoke of how his parents had refused to accept Mary and how much they had hurt John over the years through incessant devaluation of his choices, feelings, and dreams. That led Mary to (perhaps unconsciously) feel more relief than sadness over John's father's demise.

Mary explained, "I felt really protective of you and hated seeing you emotionally wither every time you were around your parents. I hated your parents for what they did to you, but I could only stand on the sidelines, helplessly watching."

She hesitated.

" . . . I'm glad your father's gone. His criticism and hostility died with him."

John also began to express sadness and relief over his father's death as he began to open up about his feelings toward each of his parents. This led us to explore John's own internal struggle to allow himself to become dependent on Mary and to trust in her love, given how disturbed his relationship had been with his parents.

Drawing on my own childhood experiences, those of several close friends, and those of former patients with similar family backgrounds, I said, "John, you have been discussing how you didn't feel emotionally safe with either of your parents and couldn't trust them. As a result, from an early age, you gave up on ever having a close and loving relationship with them and threw yourself into your studies. Do you have any thoughts about whether those early-childhood experiences influence how you relate to Mary?"

He said, "I find it really hard to trust her—to trust anyone I feel love for."

His heart had been broken by a yearning for love that had gone unmet as a child, and as a result, he was afraid to trust Mary with his heart. He wept over this realization and apologized to her.

"Mary, I'm so sorry."

"It's okay. I understand now. And I hope you can see that I'd never deliberately hurt you. I'm not like your parents. I still love you, despite everything that has happened to us."

We also uncovered that John was reluctant to ask Mary to try to meet his emotional and physical desires, because he had learned in his family of origin that people (his parents and siblings) were unresponsive to his wishes. In part, his depression had developed over his mistaken belief that he had no voice in his marriage as well and that Mary was unwilling to respond to his needs.

"John," Mary responded, "I'm willing to try to help you feel happier in any way I can. I just need to understand what you need." This positive realization began to lift his depression.

As Mary and John worked through these issues that had developed over their fifteen years of marriage, I encouraged John to reach out to Mary's children to forge a new relationship with them. We brainstormed ways to accomplish this goal. He first reached out to her older daughter and apologized to her for keeping his distance.

"I told her that I was afraid she would resent my presence and object to my role as a parent, as an authority figure. I feared that she wouldn't return the love I gave her, and I described a little about my troubled childhood and that I have difficulty with close relationships."

Mary's daughter was grateful that John reached out and apologized, admitted that she was initially jealous of her mother's relationship with him, feared losing her mom to him, and was now hopeful that they could place their relationship on a new footing. She admitted that she longed for a father figure that she could rely on.

John took a somewhat different approach with Mary's younger daughter, which also began to improve their relationship, and he finally began to feel that he and Mary had a cohesive and loving family, which now also included two grandchildren.

Over time, with patient and persistent hard work together, Mary came to understand that John's virtual affair with Cindy was due to his depression and feelings of estrangement (Cindy was a kind of antidepressant for John), and her trust in him was gradually reestablished. And as the work progressed, they became more affectionate toward each other; their sexual relations, which had once been quite satisfying but had waned in recent years, were resumed.

Our final session together took place shortly after the Thanksgiving and Christmas holidays. Both John and Mary reported that, despite some mild skirmishes, everybody had a good time at their family get-togethers, and they were able to share abundant love and warmth across three generations.

"Each of you has worked so hard in here to share your stories," I responded, "and many of the unresolved and unspoken feelings and conflicts that went along with them. You struggled to listen with empathy and curiosity, to finally understand one another. You had the courage to face up to so many painful feelings that had developed before you ever met and throughout your life together. You came to feel emotionally safe with one another and to learn that many of your conflicts were the result of misunderstandings and assumptions based on troubled childhood relationships that you carried over into this relationship.

"What each of you had assumed to be true about the other often turned out to be false. This is such an important lesson to remember when those inevitable bumps in the road come along. If you meet these conflicts head-on, with a spirit of curiosity, listening, and learning, and with empathy for one another, these deep misunderstandings can largely be prevented. I wish both of you all the best that life has to offer, and if you feel the need to come in for a tune up, please don't hesitate to call me." We hugged one another and parted ways.

* * *

The most important lesson to learn from Mary and John's story is that even severely damaged marriages or long-term committed love relationships, where the hurt began years ago, can be turned around with patience, hard work, and a willingness to listen and learn from one another.

In the last few examples, we've seen husbands and wives dealing with the damaging fallout of their *own* parents' marriages—but in those instances, the previous generations seemingly never made efforts to reverse the dysfunction in their failing relationships. Sadly, some of that has to do with the lack of availability and acceptance of couples therapy—or any therapy—in previous decades, as well as the stigma of leaving a marriage (especially for women).

But what if those parents (and grandparents) had tried to improve their relationships? Perhaps their adult children would have been spared some of their own trauma. Please consider this observation if you have children who are old enough to observe what's not working in your marriage.

Begin to Heal

If your marriage or long-term committed relationship is a dark and unhappy place, there is a lot of work to do. As we did in the therapy with John and Mary, begin by looking back to see where your love relationship went off track. As a part of this process, it is essential that both you and your partner share responsibility for the decline. Developing an atmosphere of emotional safety, understanding what went wrong and working through it, a readiness to forgive and let go of the hurt and anger, and beginning to consciously treat each other better will enable both of you to move on to something better and more gratifying. A positive momentum will develop that can increase your level of satisfaction as well as theirs.

There are steps you can take to begin to solve your issues. Please take out your workbook and begin to journal your responses to the following prompts and questions:

Step 1: How is your relationship now?

How would you characterize your marriage or other committed love relationship? Is it basically satisfying? If not, what is missing? If there are any satisfying aspects, please write them down as well.

Step 2: What went wrong?

Has the relationship gone off track? If so, when was it last good, and what was that like? What happened to derail it? Make a list of the various upsets and traumas that occurred, and next to each item, write down how it affected you and how you behaved toward each other.

Step 3: Honestly evaluate your feelings.

Have you become angry, withdrawn, depressed, coldly remote? Did you pretend to be nice while secretly hating your partner? What other feelings may underlie that anger? Disappointment? Sadness? Unmet longing? Shame or humiliation? Anxiety or fear? Provide a detailed response for each feeling. Has your behavior led you to hurt your partner? How so? Be prepared to take responsibility for your actions in an open and authentic manner.

Step 4: How have your previous relationships shaped you?

Although some of the anger and disappointment that you feel undoubtedly relates to how your partner has treated you, some of it also derives from earlier relationships where you were let down, disappointed, or betrayed. Try to examine your relationships with your parents and how they behaved toward one another, to analyze how these influences may be affecting your feelings and behavior toward your partner. Engage in self-reflection and then write down what you have learned about yourself.

Step 5: Take responsibility.

Sometimes, one partner needs to be the first to own up to their part in how the loving bonds began to deteriorate. Are you willing to step up? If not, why not? Write out your answers in your workbook. Consider gathering up your courage and sitting down with your significant other to let them know that you have been giving a lot of thought to your relationship, feel bad about how you have hurt them, and you would like to share some of the insights you have developed in the spirit of exploring the relationship and improving it.

Step 6: Face your fears.

Are you scared to take this first step? Form a mental picture of what is making you afraid, write it down, and examine it to see if it is realistic. Might the risk be worth the benefit? Are the possible outcomes any worse than how you have been feeling anyway? Write out all of the possible outcomes.

Although it may feel frightening to initiate this exploration, have the courage to believe in your conviction that the two of you can improve things. Opening up this dialogue can begin to untangle the logjam and allow the two of you to explore the origins and causes of the damage to your relationship. Write down what you believe your partner's reactions might be. List as many as possible. Then write down how you will address each of them, and run your ideas past a close friend or family member.

Step 7: Get help when necessary.

If your partner is unwilling to sit down with you, suggest that the two of you see a couples therapist. Bring up this idea empathetically: Say that you wonder if they are as unhappy in the relationship as you are. Write out any examples of ways that they have expressed their unhappiness, and bring them up if need be. Point out that the relationship is stuck, and for the two of you to feel happier, you will need to seek outside help. Couples therapy can provide first aid or even life support for your broken relationship and can enable the two of you to work through the many wounds and misunderstandings, rediscover your love, and learn new ways to resolve inevitable conflicts.

Step 8: Work on yourself.

If your partner refuses, seek individual therapy to see if you and the therapist can develop some strategies to improve the relationship, and encourage your partner to enter a dialogue with you to listen, learn, and work on a better life together. Write out an agenda of what you would like to cover with the therapist.

Step 9: When all else fails, consider moving on.

Should your partner still refuse to cooperate despite all of your best efforts, and you remain really unhappy, it is time to explore with your therapist whether ending the relationship makes sense. List the pros and cons of staying versus leaving.

Separation and divorce are big, scary steps, but the prospect of remaining deeply unfulfilled for the rest of your life is worse and may fill you with chronic depression, anger, and bitterness. That is no way to live. By getting support from your therapist, friends, and family, you can develop the courage and strength to move on with your life to a place of greater happiness.

SESSION NINE

Recovering from Empty Nest Syndrome

In an earlier session, we talked about letting go of our children as they emerge into adulthood and the emotional struggles that characterize this phase of life for them and for us as parents. Today, we are going to learn about a related issue: what it feels like when they have left home for good and how that impacts intimacy with your partner.

For many of us parents, a child is the sunshine in our lives from the moment they are born. At their birth, a new kind of love emerges from within us, bringing qualities that never existed before. We immediately feel a deep need to protect and care for our infant—an awesome responsibility—and may be filled with yearning for who they will become.

There are the many firsts—first smile, first "Mama" and "Dada," first time sleeping through the night, first birthday party, first steps, first high fever that wakes us in the middle of the night, first day of school, first soccer goal, first time riding a bike, then driving a car—each of which is special in its own way. Each child goes through a phase where they experience virtually every new experience with a kind of delight in their face, and we are able to share in that joyfulness. These are the magic years of discovery, when we begin to help them explore the world and when they seem like little sponges that absorb almost everything we teach them.

Not uncommonly, we become the most important people in their life, which can feel wonderful. Each event that we share with them may create a deeper emotional attachment.

Then come the teenage years, which usher in the end of an era, as our children turn more toward their friends, distance themselves from us in preparation for leaving home, and become more challenging in how they relate.

During the first two decades following the birth of a child, many couples focus almost exclusively on raising their family and achieving career success. Unseen—or, at best, dimly perceived—is the damage being done to their love relationship, which has been neglected. Like a once lovely garden whose flowers wither and die from insufficient care and feeding, loving feelings may perish as well.

As a result of our children leaving the nest, clouds may gather over our hearts as the sunshine they once provided now fades away. We may long to return to a time when they were little kids filled with the joy of discovery or to reconnect with old lovers or to discover a new love and feel young again.

♪ **Session Soundtrack** ♪

The song "More Than a Feeling," by the rock band Boston, touchingly depicts someone who wakes up one morning to find that "the sun is gone," turns on an old and familiar song, and slips away into memories of people who have come and gone and of a girl he used to love. He hides in the music to forget the day. And then the memories and faces begin to fade away.

The song "Ditmas" by the British rock band Mumford & Sons provides another relevant description of a life made elusive by its fast pace, a broken house, empty words, and a couple once in love, who are losing one another after years of being together. The singer wonders if there is another way. These are powerful feelings that can overcome us as we face the reality of our children growing up and leaving home. And these feelings can have a profound effect on our marriage or other committed love relationship.

Visit DrBruceKehr.com/music-8 for audio files
and further discussion of the soundtracks.

Many of the couples that I treat present in a crisis triggered by **empty nest syndrome**. There is a common thread to their stories: Both husband and wife have been driven to succeed at work and in raising their kids. They strive to provide the best possible life for their children—an excellent education, active engagement in sports and other extracurricular activities, a full social life, tutoring support for challenging courses and SAT preparation—to prepare their kids for an increasingly complex and competitive world. For those mothers or fathers who stay at home, this becomes nearly a full-time occupation and is an important source of commitment and pride. At the same time, one or both parents are climbing the career ladder to achieve the tangible and intangible rewards that come with professional success.

What not infrequently gets neglected, what often gets pushed aside, is a comparable level of dedication, energy, drive, and commitment to their life partner. All too often, the last child leaving for college is a wakeup call, and the couple is suddenly alone at home, facing one other for the first time in many years. For some, there is the frightening realization that they live with a virtual stranger. There may be a corresponding awareness of the end of an era, one that had been filled with sports team events, plays, dance recitals, memorable teachers, PTA meetings, and summer camp experiences, and a sad farewell to that cast of supporting characters you shared these events with—all of the other kids, parents, and professionals that made for such richly rewarding experiences.

There may be a painful awareness that you and your partner have drifted apart, have become "emotionally divorced," with emotional and physical intimacy a distant memory. This may also coincide with increasing mindfulness of your own mortality and other issues that accompany a midlife crisis.

A depression may set in, along with a yearning to feel young again and to relive an earlier phase of life. Memories may return of prior love relations, along with fantasies of a happier life with a different choice of partner. This may fill you with despair, longing, and regret. But these are feelings you can work through together to regain your lost love.

Todd and Nancy's Story

Todd and Nancy entered therapy around his escalating anger outbursts at home, particularly on weekends, and her resulting fear, emotional isolation, and estrangement. He was a senior executive at a global technology company, and she was a homemaker active in various volunteer positions at charitable organizations. Todd would fly off the handle at seemingly minor mishaps, such as misplacing his cellphone or having technical problems with his computer, and would not uncommonly destroy the offending technology in a fit of rage while frightening Nancy, who feared that he might strike her as well. She was passive and afraid to set limits on his behavior and therefore suffered in silence.

"While I love him very much," she said in our first session, "and enjoy his wonderful sense of humor, unless he can control his anger, I'll have to file for separation and divorce."

"I have a lot of pressure at work," Todd said. "I'm trying to cope with the intense stress involved in running a company. The recession has hit us hard, and it's accelerating change in our industry that I'm trying to keep ahead of."

However, Nancy didn't believe that explanation. "Todd, you typically thrive on this sort of challenge. You've always taken pride in facing challenges and successfully leading the company.

"I think the real issue behind your anger is more about our empty nest." The last of their four children had recently left home to attend college, and their other three kids had moved out of state and were less engaged with the family.

Todd initially resisted this notion. However, in our third couples session, this powerful executive began to openly weep about his oldest daughter having moved to San Francisco to assume a new and demanding position as an attorney, which prevented her from attending the traditional family summer vacation for the first time. It was bittersweet.

"I'm immensely proud of her," he said. "But I long for the good old days, when she was an integral part of family events filled with fun and warmth. I never had an experience like that with my own parents." Todd's family of origin had been fraught with emotional distance, frequent parental fighting, and a highly critical and demanding father.

As Todd was speaking, I recalled what it felt like when our two daughters first went away to sleepaway camp: like someone had ripped my heart out of my chest. My wife and I missed them so much, and it had felt depressing. When our first and then our second daughter went away to college, we were excited for them but felt our hearts break. It was the end of an era; our daily family closeness would be gone forever. I had wept in secret each time my wife and I had said goodbye to our daughters, as we left them behind in their dorm rooms.

"Todd," I said, "it is understandable that your heart feels broken and that you miss your kids so much. As proud as you may feel about their moving on in life, you may also feel sad and angry and are grieving inside. You may be displacing some of these feelings onto Nancy. Are you aware of these feelings and how deeply you hold them?"

"This is the first time I've been aware of this. I didn't realize I was grieving. It feels good to be able to share these feelings."

Adding to Todd's sense of loss, while the nest was emptying out, Todd had a much stronger sexual attraction toward Nancy than she did toward him. Her own libido had diminished as she mourned the loss of her active mothering, felt less attractive, went through menopause, and found Todd increasingly unattractive because he behaved in ways that frightened her. Struggling with her own feelings of grief and fear, Nancy had turned off her desires for sexual intimacy, which would have helped Todd feel more desired by her and reinforced his sexual prowess at a time when he felt increasingly powerless over his children moving on. His anger drove Nancy away, which, in turn, made him feel abandoned and even angrier. It was a cycle that we needed to explore and understand, because Todd had begun openly threatening that he would have an affair with a younger woman, angrily blaming Nancy for his urges to cheat on her.

For Nancy's part, she said, "Your frightening behavior was

frustrating and disappointing. And threatening to cheat on me! How would I not be turned off by that?"

To add a little humor to these sad and conflict-ridden sessions, I helped Todd understand Nancy's feelings by telling a story from an episode of the popular TV series *Justified*. In one of the episodes, our hero, Deputy US Marshall Raylan Givens, has separated from his wife and is living above a bar, where a beautiful blonde bartender serves drinks. Raylan, who is quite handsome and sexy, tries to seduce her, and her response was (I'm paraphrasing) "Raylan, when it comes to sex, men and women are quite different. All men need is a place. Women need a reason."

Todd and Nancy were able to laugh at this truism, and it helped to cut the tension and have them begin to discuss some additional concerns brought on by their recently emptied nest.

"I didn't realize I was so afraid of growing older," Todd began. "I don't want to grow feeble like my parents and Nancy's did."

Both Todd's and Nancy's parents had also passed away in recent years. These feelings were amplified as Todd considered the youth of his children and the announcement by his twenty-five-year-old son that he would be asking his attractive and successful young girlfriend for her hand in marriage.

I commented, "Nancy, you are understandably upset over Todd's angry threats to cheat on you, but perhaps now we can put them in context and also help him to understand what you have been living through. Todd is clearly struggling with fears around getting older and dying. These feelings have been heightened by the loss of his parents and yours over the past five years, because he loved each of them very much. Todd has deep yearnings to feel young again, which are partly satisfied through having sexual relations with you. He still finds you attractive, and sex with you makes him feel more youthful and alive. This doesn't excuse his threatening behaviors.

But does it help you to put them in context in a way that makes him more human?"

She nodded in assent.

"Nancy, would you mind sharing what this phase of life means for you, to help Todd understand what you have been feeling inside?"

"My heart aches," she said, "over losing my role in the lives of my children. And I've been going through menopause and the physical, emotional, and sexual changes that come with it."

She described with deep sadness how, for many years, she would lovingly prepare and serve meals to the six of them. "I'd look out over the family dinner table each evening, feeling love and pride. Now this phase of my life is gone forever."

Through the course of these sessions, both Todd and Nancy began to reach a deeper understanding of their previously hidden emotional pain, and they began to empathize with one another and share the losses they had jointly experienced. Over time, they stopped blaming each other as the cause of their unhappiness. To fill that empty nest, Nancy and Todd began to rediscover a love of travel they had shared in the early days of their marriage, before the children came along. They frequently Skyped and texted with their kids to more actively participate in their lives, made a point of deepening the ties to their children's spouses, and were now eagerly anticipating a first grandchild.

To reestablish their friendship, Todd and Nancy would take long walks several times each week. They would talk for an hour or so, emotionally connecting and providing support for one other. They began exploring some of the more intimate, romantic res-taurants around town. As the anger and tension in their relation-ship dissipated, their sex life was rekindled, and they rediscovered their feelings of attraction for one another. In our final session, they were both filled with immense excitement, anticipating becoming grandparents in the very near future. Their once empty nest was now bursting with new life.

The story of Todd and Nancy illustrates how life had overtaken them in a way that was beyond their conscious awareness. They each felt deep emotional pain over the passing of an era and blamed the other for their feelings, which were largely unconscious and actually had to do with their stage of life.

Begin to Heal

The empty nest era may provoke an internal crisis and can seriously strain your marriage or other committed love relationship. However, there are a number of steps a couple can take to prevent this from happening. Please write down your responses to the following prompts and questions in your workbook:

Step 1: Find ways to emotionally connect with one another.

If your children are younger and still living at home, ask yourself the following questions, and be brutally honest with yourself: Do you feel love and affection for your partner? If not, what are you feeling toward them? Do you like them? If not, what don't you like about them? Is there a friendship? If so, how would you characterize it? Do you have fun together without the kids? If not, write out three ways that the two of you could have fun together. Do you get sitters and go out on dates—just the two of you—to reconnect? If not, what are the obstacles, and how might they be overcome? Do you ever vacation without the kids? If not, why not, and how might you arrange for this type of trip?

Step 2: Nurture your relationship.

It is vital that you tend to your love relationship with the same level of devotion that you give to parenting and your career. Is this the case? If not, list three immediate steps that you could take to make your love relationship top priority. Formally schedule time together with your partner, just as you would schedule attendance at a soccer game or school play. Find a reliable babysitter or offer to trade services with friends or family members to enable the two of you to get out, get reacquainted, have fun, and laugh together. Who might you approach to trade services? List the positives and negatives of each potential choice.

These seemingly simple steps may feel hard to carry out when you are in the thick of it, raising your kids and tending to your career, but they are vital to maintaining or restoring a strong bond between you and your partner.

Step 3: Discuss your feelings about the transition.

If your children recently left home, it is important to explicitly acknowledge the end of that era and this new phase of life that you and your partner are entering. Talk together about your sense of loss around your children moving out and moving on. Write down at least five feelings that you have about the change and some details about why you feel that way, and be willing to share these with your partner to encourage them to share as well.

Step 4: Mourn your empty nest.

Actively reminisce about your lives together when the kids lived at home. Think back to some funny moments when they made both of you laugh. Recall some of the trips that you took with fondness. Talk about the idiosyncrasies and quirks in their personalities and when you first noticed them. Recall times when they brought their friends over and what was shared with them. List at least five wonderful memories and share them with your partner. This can help to ease the pain of separation and loss, help you feel less alone with your feelings, and help emotionally connect you and your partner.

If you feel relief that the difficult teenagers that were living at home are now away at college, write down at least three ways that you feel relieved, and be willing to share these as well.

Step 5: Revel in your freedom!

This life stage can bring about a newfound sense of independence that can be both exhilarating and a bit bewildering, at least at first. What are three ways that you and your partner can celebrate your freedom? What dreams have been put off while raising your kids? Please write out your ideas and then share them.

Step 6: Reclaim what you gave up to become a parent.

Reminisce about activities you enjoyed together before you had children—such as travel, particular restaurants, dancing, and sports—and see if you might enjoy rediscovering them. What are five stories that come to mind that bring a smile to your face that you are willing to reminisce about with your partner? Please list them here, and then go share them!

Travel, actively seek entertainment or recreational activities, and visit friends in distant cities. This is also an opportunity to rediscover old hobbies that were once individually rewarding and to jointly discover new pursuits that can rebuild an emotional connection. Arrange for you and your partner to list five pursuits that you had previously shared that may be worth rediscovering, and share them with one another.

Step 7: Commit to rebuilding your relationship.

Be willing to dedicate the same level of diligent work to rebuilding your relationship that was devoted to climbing up the career ladder and supporting your children during their formative years. What are you willing to commit to this endeavor? Please write it down to share with your partner.

Step 8: Actively focus on and discuss your relationship.

List five important issues or conflicts that you and your partner should talk about in the near future, along with your feelings about each topic and ways that the two of you may resist talking about them. If you don't talk with one another, you are at higher risk of separation and divorce or of remaining involved in a relationship that is stagnant and breeds loneliness. A consistent focus on rebuilding what was once satisfying can bring about a newly enriched life together.

Step 9: Treat each other well.

Work hard to treat each other with kindness and listen respectfully. What are four ways that you could act more kindly toward your life partner? List the ways that you would like them to treat you more kindly as well.

Step 10: Congratulate one another.

Give yourselves credit for all of your hard work, and express appreciation to one another for the ways that you have devoted yourselves to raising your children. Whether it was patiently listening to stories that would never end, having to be tough on enforcing the rules, working extra hours to afford summer camp or visits to the orthodontist, or all of the many ways you each contributed to their growth and development, congratulate one another! Write out at least eight ways the two of you have sacrificed to raise your children, and be willing to talk about them with a sense of shared pride.

Step 11: Lay your fears aside.

Although you may well feel reluctant to try these techniques, may feel skeptical that they will make any difference, or may believe that your partner will disparage them, try out one or two of them. Which one or two are you willing to try first? Write out any fears that are holding you back, and really question how valid they are. You may surprise yourself with how some positive feelings may begin to return.

Step 12: Feel sad *and* find the positives.

Take a hard look at yourself in the mirror, and recognize that both you and your partner are facing life stage issues that may feel daunting. Growing older, health concerns, waning power and influence, feeling less attractive, and more fully recognizing your mortality— all in the context of your youthful children launching their own lives—can be emotionally painful. It is a bittersweet time of life, as you feel happy for them and proud of the sacrifices you made that helped them reach this moment. And yet, at the same time, you may struggle with fears of growing older, long to be young again, and feel envious of your child. List five positive attributes of this new phase of your life that were not possible when your children were young.

Step 13: Get help when you need it.

If these techniques are not helpful and you are stuck in an emotionally painful place, it is important that you seek help. Before throwing in the towel, commit to six months of couples therapy, or individual therapy if your partner refuses couples work. Write down in some detail your top five concerns, to enable you to share them with the therapist.

Therapy will help clarify the underlying unresolved issues and will assist you in working toward a resolution. If the decision is to end the marriage or long-term committed love relationship, you can look your children in the eye and say that you did everything you could prior to reaching your decision.

Heal the Mutilating Effects of Trauma and Find Self-Love

Session Ten

Trauma and Intimate Relationships

So far in our sessions together, we've moved chronologically through life stages, from childhood to adulthood, learning about and reflecting on ways to heal and become whole at any age. Now, I want to talk with you about experiences that transcend any one age or era in our lives. The aftereffects of trauma, especially childhood sexual abuse, can live deep inside our hearts and minds for our entire lives. These lingering effects can be all pervasive and ruinous to each and every relationship in our lives. This is a most difficult topic for us to cover. But as we explore it, I'll be at your side.

As you know from our work in session 7, the establishment of intimate emotional relationships is crucial to our well-being. In that session, I discussed the many ways we hold ourselves back from establishing the level of intimacy necessary for mature adult love. In the next two sessions, we will explore together how childhood trauma affects the development of intimate bonds later in our lives. Whether or not you or someone you love has been a trauma victim or has survived childhood sexual abuse, the lessons taught through the stories of Tara and Brad will probably touch you deeply and will teach you a great deal about how our human hearts respond to any serious trauma. And, hopefully, through them, you will learn more about yourself. After all, how many of us live a life untouched by at least some significant trauma?

Our capacity for intimacy begins in childhood, as we establish early emotional bonds with our mother and father. Typically, these first experiences with another human being have a profound influence on our emotional development and our later capacities to form intimate relationships. For some of us, these parent–child bonds may be rock solid, trustworthy, and secure, in which case, our capacity for intimacy in adult life will be well developed and stable.

For others, during the course of our childhood, our parents may be unavailable, inconsistent, self-absorbed, emotionally volatile, or physically or sexually abusive. In these instances, our capacity for later-life intimacy will be damaged. In adult life, these emotional wounds may be expressed in a number of ways as our desire for a stable love relationship comes into conflict with our fear of commitment, feelings of mistrust, and fragile self-esteem that form the residue of the damaging relations of childhood.

It's helpful to begin to look back on your life to discover what has influenced your ability to love. As you do so, whether in therapy or as part of your self-reflection, you may come to find the many ways in which the effects of childhood trauma can linger on in your life. For example, as a result of damaging childhood, adolescent, or adult relationships, a **repetition compulsion**[1] may develop: This compulsion drives us to unconsciously repeat earlier traumas time and time again through patterns of self-sabotaging behavior in love relationships. These unconscious behaviors may interfere with or destroy intimate bonds. Feelings of love and tenderness may develop, but difficulty trusting and fear of expressing these emotions directly complicate the relationship.

This type of self-sabotage is exemplified in the young-adult woman who hooks up with a series of (often older) men in a futile attempt to find emotional closeness and love and affection that never developed with her father. This can also be a way to feel power over men by first seducing and then abandoning them. The young man who engages in a series of hookups to prove his prowess and gain narcissistic gratification does so because of self-esteem problems that began as a child. Perhaps he felt powerless in his relationship with his mother or father, or perhaps a deeper trauma occurred. Unmet longings for love, shame, and humiliation and deep feelings of helplessness resulting from traumatic experiences in earlier relationships are not uncommonly expressed (unconsciously) through many forms of self-sabotage of later intimate relations.

Psychoanalytic psychotherapy can be very helpful in uncovering and resolving the unconscious causes of repeated failed relationships and the difficulties in establishing or maintaining intimacy that result from child abuse or later-life traumas, such as rape. The therapist engages the patient in a caring and trusting relationship, encourages the patient to free associate about their thoughts, feelings, fantasies, and memories related to the current and earlier love relationships, and over time, the unconscious conflicts that damage intimate relations emerge. Both the therapist and the patient need to commit to a longer-term therapy to work through the emerging issues that interfere with intimacy, because the earlier traumatic experiences and emotional conflicts exert a tenacious hold over the patient's emotional life.

Sticking with therapy can become quite challenging. At times, it involves emotionally painful sessions as the patient intensely relives the emotions surrounding earlier traumatic relations. As we discussed in an earlier session, this process is called **abreaction**.[2] The therapeutic method uncovers prior conflicted relationships that damaged feelings of closeness and intimacy and the development of trust. It repeatedly exposes the patient to the emotional confusion and distress that they experienced at those times. The patient grieves the loss of what had been desired but that remained unfulfilled, learns how to tolerate and bear the intense emotional reactions (as opposed to running away or acting them out[3]), and comes to understand and put into perspective the reasons for the earlier disappointments.

This process enables the patient to let go of the traumatic experiences, which gradually lose their hold over the patient's emotional life, bringing with it a freedom to experience healthier adult love. It is very gratifying for the therapist to see their patient emerge from this process happily engaged in a more mature love, with their heart finally released from the emotional bonds created by past traumas.

What is learned in therapy will hopefully be applied time and again over the course of our lifetime, because emotional intimacy is fragile.

The following story illustrates why anyone who has suffered from the aftereffects of sexual or physical abuse would have difficulty establishing an intimate emotional relationship and would be emotionally paralyzed, in a way, from moving forward. It also shows the value of exploring each of the disturbing details of what was done to the victim with a caring and empathetic therapist.

The national statistics on abuse are astounding.[4] About one in ten children will be sexually abused prior to their eighteenth birthday (one in seven girls and one in twenty-five boys). And about 20 million women have been raped during their lifetime; this is 18 percent of the adult woman population in the United States. Around 44 percent of rapes with penetration occur in children under the age of eighteen. Most (90 percent) of children who have been sexually abused know the perpetrator, and approximately 30 percent were abused by a family member. Fully half of the abusers who molested a child under six were family members. These statistics make Tara's story especially important.

Whether they are victimized by childhood sexual abuse or raped as a college student, the survivor is overwhelmed by many confusing and contradictory emotions and feels alone in trying to cope with them. They describe the immediate aftereffects as feeling emotionally overwhelmed and paralyzed and express how difficult it is to stay afloat each and every day. Perhaps the most painful are the feelings of shame and humiliation, but much of this aloneness can be healed through sharing anything and everything with a caring and empathetic therapist, which we will learn much more about as the stories of Tara—and in the next session, Brad—unfold.

Tara's Story

Tara was a senior IT project manager at a large defense contractor and was forty years old when she came to me asking for help with a number of areas in her life: She was experiencing increasing anger outbursts at work. Her self-esteem had plummeted, and she drank to excess in the evenings. She had gained weight and felt that she was chronically emotionally distant from her husband, something she felt particularly guilty about as he was recovering from surgery for prostate cancer. She was also depressed and wondered whether she suffered from ADHD. Her history and current symptoms supported the diagnosis of persistent depressive disorder (a chronic, low-grade form of depression) and attention deficit disorder without hyperactivity, both of which respond well to medication.

To treat Tara under the biopsychosocial model, it would be necessary to address the underlying neurobiology of her emotional distress, as well as her impulsive behavior, marital problems, and chronically low self-esteem. Recall that in our very first session, I discussed how talk therapy, medication, and certain nutritional interventions can turn on and restore the body's naturally protective mechanisms (so-called epigenetic influences[5]), which may, in turn, restore normal energy production and connectivity among brain cells. In Tara's story, you will see firsthand how medication management will be interwoven with psychological factors to treat her as a **whole person**, rather than simply treating her with medication or addressing only one aspect of her emotional problems.

At the end of our initial session, I walked Tara through what I felt would be the most effective strategies to help her heal and informed her that these were based on my years of experience successfully treating other patients who had suffered from problems similar to hers. By providing Tara an initial game plan, including the rationale behind it, I began to fill her with some hope among her deep feelings of hopelessness.

"Tara, broadly speaking, we will pursue two strategies in our work together. The first involves treating the underlying biological basis of your depression and ADHD. We can use medication to increase the levels of dopamine and norepinephrine in the circuits of your brain that support attentional and executive functioning and mood regulation. There are additional ways to improve these circuits, including a reduction in your alcohol consumption, improving your diet, regular cardiovascular exercise, and judicious use of certain nutritional supplements—all of which can be discussed at a later time, if you like.

"The second strategy involves exploring the unconscious causes of your need to emotionally distance yourself from your husband. This will involve us meeting once a week for talk therapy and developing a deeper understanding of your most important childhood relationships and how they affect your ability to love. How do these recommendations sound to you?"

Tara liked this approach, and we began our work together.

I prescribed Wellbutrin, which can help improve both depressive and ADHD symptoms, because it increases dopamine and norepinephrine levels in the frontal lobe and other regions of the brain, which may improve mood, attention, working memory,[6] and concentration. It can also help reduce appetite, which would support the weight-loss program we devised for Tara, reducing simple carbohydrates and processed foods, increasing the consumption of wild fish and fruits and vegetables, and taking omega 3 fish oil.[7]

We then began to explore her childhood. Tara grew up in France, in an upper-middle-class professional family. She experienced an emotionally troubled home life; her mother and father were unhappily married.

"My father was a successful attorney," she said. "He drank a lot but hid it from the outside world. At home, he'd fly into violent rages. He never hit me, but he often threatened to. And he would shout horrible things at my mother."

In turn, her mother, a beautiful, emotionally dramatic woman, made no secret of the fact that she had a lover. "At times, she'd taunt my father, provoking him. I was always afraid he'd strike her—or worse."

"How did you feel growing up?" I asked.

"I felt utterly alone, unwanted, and frightened by my father's rage."

Neither of Tara's parents provided what is known as an emotional **safe base**—a feeling that develops within the child that both mother and father will be a stable and reliable source of emotional safety.[8] Through repeated experiences of emotional safety, the child begins to establish trust and feels comforted, understood, responded to, cared for, and protected. Without a safe base, a child may grow up feeling emotionally isolated, that they don't belong in their family (or in the world at all), and they may suffer from an inability to form deep bonds of trust later in life.

I said to her, "Tara, from what you are describing, it is no wonder that you have difficulty with emotional intimacy. It wasn't emotionally safe for you to get close to either of your parents. Your father was a frightening figure, and your mother was excessively self-absorbed. You couldn't trust either of them with your feelings, and so you became self-reliant at an early age. In part, this fierce self-reliance has served you well in the business world, but it doesn't serve you so well at home. You have described your husband as a loving, emotionally mature, and available man, yet you keep a distance from him. Mistrusting him is clearly a factor here. Are there other relationships from childhood that may have influenced your capacity to trust, or do you believe that it principally relates to your relations with your mother and father?"

Tara thought about this question for a minute or so and then reported, "When I was fourteen years old, my parents sent me away to a coed boarding school. I initially felt a great sense of relief. I made friends easily, I was a good athlete and a bright student, and the headmaster of the school took a fatherly interest in me. I really liked the headmaster, who seemed so cultured and worldly, so warm and friendly.

"From the very first moment that I met him, I wished that the headmaster was my real father. He would invite me to his office for special tutoring sessions, offer me assignments for extra credit, and generally treat me in a caring, friendly, and interested fashion. I opened up to him and poured my heart out about how unhappy I had been at home and how happy I now felt at the school. He would frequently tell me what a special young lady I was, that I was exceptionally smart, that all of my teachers really liked me, and that I was one of the finest students they had ever taught at the school. He also repeatedly told me how pretty I was."

This flattery made Tara feel very special. It was so different from what she had experienced at home with her parents that she lapped it up, and so she looked forward to the time she spent with the headmaster.

Sadly, two years later, around the time Tara turned sixteen, the relationship turned sexual. The headmaster first began by kissing Tara on the cheek and then on her lips, while telling her she was so pretty. Later on, he began to fondle her breasts and tell her what a special young woman she was. Ultimately, he seduced her, and they had sexual intercourse on three occasions.

"He said I couldn't tell anyone, because it would mean that I couldn't stay at the school anymore and would have to return home. That possibility would make me feel worse than what he and I were doing, so I didn't say anything. I was forced to carry this terrible secret inside me. I thought about killing myself, but I couldn't. I just let him take what he wanted."

As she recounted this story, Tara looked sad and ashamed. I said to her, "Tara, I deeply appreciate the confidence and trust that you have placed in me in sharing what he did to you. When you feel ready—and there is no pressure or urgency in this—I would like to understand what you were feeling at the time and how you feel about it now."

"You're the first person in my entire life I've shared any of this with," she said. "I put up with it for just over a year. Then, fortunately, the headmaster left the school."

She eventually became one of the top students at the school and graduated with honors. She went on to study computer science and earned a Top Secret clearance, which enabled her to work on extremely sensitive projects related to national security. Tara married at age thirty and gave birth to three children.

Although she enjoyed career success and was admired and respected by her subordinates, her home life was troubled and was causing her a great deal of emotional pain. Her husband complained that he felt lonely in the marriage and felt abandoned by her in raising their three children, one of whom was having serious emotional problems.

Tara's twelve-year-old son, Carey, had a violent temper and mood swings and was possibly drinking alcohol and smoking marijuana. He was rude and disrespectful at home and was beginning to have behavioral problems at school. Tara felt great pain over these family problems.

"Before my first child was born," she said, "I vowed that their lives would be markedly different from mine, that my children would grow up feeling loved and safe."

"Tara, unlike your mother or father, you care deeply about each of your children's lives, and the love you feel for them is palpable. Let's arrange for a child and family therapist to consult with you and your husband regarding Carey."

Tara and her husband entered family therapy, and Carey began specialized treatment (dialectical behavioral therapy, or DBT),[9] which involved individual and group therapy. Tara felt some relief and hope that her family situation would begin to improve. We could now focus more on her issues with intimacy.

We began to address Tara's feelings toward her parents. Through exploring her longing for a closer relationship with them, fears of being attacked by her father, and deep disappointment regarding her mother's self-absorption, we were able to establish a therapeutic relationship built on trust and mutual respect. Although this work was arduous, because Tara was unaccustomed to recognizing, experiencing, and communicating her feelings, it turned out to be the easier work.

"In many respects," she said at one point, "I had left my parents long ago. I had to become independent at an early age, given how alone I had felt at home."

We then began working on her memories of having been sexually exploited and the resulting scars that were indelibly imprinted on her. Filled with feelings of shame, she had difficulty looking me in the eye as she wondered aloud, "Why did I keep going back to his office?"

"Tara, I interpret your actions as a deep need for a caring and loving father who would show an interest in you, which your own father didn't provide. The headmaster knew just how to manipulate you, just where you were most vulnerable. This was reprehensible behavior on his part—not yours—and it damaged your ability to trust."

Tara clenched her shaking fists, and tears welled in her eyes. "It still makes me so angry," she said. "And I feel ashamed and humiliated that I could allow myself to be treated like that."

At the end of each session, she made a point of thanking me. I would warmly respond and look her straight in the eye, hoping that, in some small way, this would help her restore her self-respect.

At times, she would develop strong feelings of anger toward me, an example of transference (see page 16). More than once, she got really angry, feeling that I didn't understand what she was thinking and feeling. She would yell at me and then feel remorse.

I explained, "Tara, the anger you feel toward me likely represents feelings you have had for others in your life as well—other important relationships where you felt misunderstood. Does anyone come to mind?"

"My parents, maybe. They never understood or loved me. They fought all the time and sent me away. They sent me to *him*.

"I get angry with Carey, too," she said. "I feel like I try so hard to do what's right for him, and he takes advantage of and manipulates me."

Sometimes, she would become suspicious of my motives, at one point saying, "You are just in it for the money. You don't really care about me; you are just using me to help pay for your daughters' college educations." At these times, she would continue by talking about the headmaster, who had feigned caring for her just to take advantage of and sexually exploit her.

I admired her courage in coming in week after week to discuss these painful and shameful events. It was easy for me to respect her, a way of being with her that she began to internalize,[10] and she began to regain respect for herself, realizing that she had been a little girl starved for love in a loveless family and that, with each encounter with the headmaster, she had been desperately seeking the love that she had longed for from her mother and father.

Tara began to feel less angry, depressed, and humiliated. Her marriage slowly began to improve, and the DBT and family therapy effectively addressed the issues with Carey. She took a six-month break from therapy to "try out her wings" and returned for a medication management visit. She had much positive news to report.

"I feel much closer to my husband," she said. "Carey is discussing his feelings with us instead of acting them out. I shared some—but not all—of my own troubled youth with him, trying to show how I empathize with what he's going through. I haven't had a drink in months. I'm much happier, but I know that there's a great deal of family therapy yet to come. For the first time in years, I think we're going to be okay."

I struggled to find a way to communicate my pride in a caring and compassionate fashion, without patronizing or embarrassing her. It is sometimes like this that the psychoanalyzed psychotherapist can reach deep inside themselves to locate memories and feelings (those countertransference reactions) that facilitate comments that heal. Recalling a theme in my own psychoanalysis about how hard I was working to create a better family life for my own family in comparison with the one in which I grew up, I said to her, "Tara, your persistent devotion to your family and your own personal growth has really begun to pay off. I am so happy for you. You have worked through a great deal of emotional pain along the way. As a result, you have ended the cycle of self-destructive behavior and transformed yourself into a patient and loving mother and wife. You are now willing to listen, learn, and understand, as opposed to reacting with anger, distancing yourself, and drinking to excess. Through our work together and your own introspection, you have developed the necessary tools to continue to grow. Let's consider this phase of our work complete, and we can move on to simply monitoring your medication every three to six months. At the same time, Tara, my door is always open if you feel the need to come back to work on any other issues in the future."

Begin to Heal

Now let's begin to work on your own capacity for an intimate emotional relationship, keeping in mind some of the issues and themes that we uncovered earlier about early-childhood relationships and trauma. Use your workbook to write your responses, going step by step to think this through.

Step 1: Assess your capacity for emotional intimacy.

How have you been doing in establishing and maintaining emotional intimacy with others? What's gone well and what hasn't? What is your capacity to trust?

If you have sustained close and loving relationships, describe each of these relationships (past and present). What has worked well? Where are the problem areas?

Have you had a series of relationships that only went so far, then dissolved as they began to become more real? Is there a pattern here? If so, please describe it.

Step 2: How do your love relationships evolve?

Maintaining a close loving relationship over time is one of the greatest challenges in life. Few of us grew up in households with parental relationships that were consistently loving, stable, and enduring. Begin to explore within yourself the various love relationships in your life, beginning in childhood, and write them down. How did each one evolve? What went well? Where were the problems? Are you conscious of any traumatic experiences? If so, please describe them in detail.

Step 3: Look for patterns.

Is there a pattern to the problems that develop in your intimate relationships? For example, do you repeatedly choose lovers with similar personality traits? Please describe any patterns in as much detail as possible.

Step 4: Raising red flags.

If you have a relationship that deteriorated, were there red flags that were visible well before the relationship stalled or ended? List some of the troubling signs. For example, how was your partner at listening and being there for you when you were talking about something important to you? Were they able to offer empathy? Compassion? How would you describe their emotional development, their availability to be with you? Were they someone who would bring out the best in you, or were they generally critical? What was their effect on your self-esteem? Perhaps you unconsciously select someone to love who is narcissistic and unable to commit, which may relate to your own fears of commitment or to personality attributes of your mother or father.

Step 5: Assess your own responses to being loved.

Is there a pattern whereby you select caring partners and then begin to feel bored with them or find some other reason to distance yourself? Do you initially feel excited, and then once you feel a bit vulnerable and dependent, you break off the relationship or find some other way to sabotage the development of intimacy? Would you misinterpret loving or caring acts as efforts to control you or tell you what to do? Would your mind stray to someone else who was more exciting yet was unable to make or sustain a commitment or who would repeatedly disappoint you?

If your answer is yes to one or more of these questions, something within you is interfering with unfolding a deeper, more meaningful relationship with a loving partner. You may have unresolved issues relating to dependency, vulnerability, and trust. These may have originated in trauma.

Step 8: Describe your early-childhood relations.

Begin to recall your own childhood experiences with your mother and your father. How would you characterize them? Did either of your parents provide you an emotional safe base? How would you describe your emotional experiences with each parent? Would you characterize either of them as physically or emotionally abusive? Please provide as many details as you can remember.

Step 9: Have you had recurring, disturbing dreams?

As a child, were there any recurring dreams or recurring themes in your dreams? What were they? Any recurring nightmares? If so, did they involve you being attacked? What clues might they provide about how you were feeling about yourself, your life, and the important relationships in your family? It's possible that you were abused and have repressed the memories of the event. Do you have a sibling who might remember? How would you feel about asking them?

Step 10: Do loved ones remind you of your parents?

As you look at the people you have chosen to love, ask yourself whether they share attributes with your mother or father and, if so, which ones? If there is a resemblance, perhaps some of the unresolved anger and disappointment that you feel toward your parents is being taken out on loved ones in your present life.

Step 11: Look even further back.

Think about the quality of the relationships that your parents and others you have loved had with *their own parents*, and write down your understanding. If you are uncertain about their childhood relationships and feel it is not too intrusive, ask them to tell you the details. (If your parents are no longer alive, seek out others in their circle whose opinions you trust and who may be able to recall details.) This exercise will help you appreciate their own internal emotional struggles.

Step 12: Look for patterns again.

Review your answers to the questions above to try to detect some patterns of behavior. Once you become conscious of repetitive self-sabotaging behaviors and the origins of some of these patterns, you can begin to develop a deeper understanding that will help you to untangle your heart. Connect the dots, and you may begin to end the patterns that sabotage your happiness.

Step 13: How can you improve?

Translate these insights into a written list of behaviors that will improve your intimate relations. Begin with a commitment to stop specific behaviors that are destructive. Then identify new behaviors that will make your partner feel special and loved, and begin to carry them out.

Step 14: Be grateful.

Write out a gratitude list of what you feel grateful for in the relationship, and add one new item to the list each day.

Step 15: Assess yourself honestly.

Finally, ask yourself a really difficult question: Am I capable of fully loving and trusting another human being? Or is this something that I resist and avoid, where I never fully commit my heart? Issues surrounding basic trust complicate many love relationships. It may feel really scary to look yourself in the eye and answer this question honestly, because the implications are profound if the answer is "no." And yet, if this is where you land, there is hope for a better future. Your mistrust and fear of deep emotional intimacy can be resolved through a longer term, insight-oriented psychodynamic psychotherapy or psychoanalysis, particularly if you are a survivor of childhood sexual or physical abuse.

The benefits of longer-term therapy were illustrated in Tara's story. Although this type of treatment can be quite expensive, if you live in a city with a training institute, significantly discounted fees are available. You can be treated by a talented trainee who is supervised by a senior psychotherapist.

SESSION ELEVEN

Transcending Sexual Abuse

Tara first lived through an emotionally abusive childhood, then through sexual abuse as a teenager. Many of the themes we discussed in her story and therapy also relate to someone who has been raped as an adolescent or young adult, such as the lingering effects on the establishment of emotional intimacy. Now it is time to explore something even more shocking and disturbing: the effects of childhood sexual abuse and its many manifestations in later adult life. You will learn about it in the story of Brad. This will be a tough session, but, as always, I will remain your companion throughout.

Childhood sexual abuse creates profound emotional conflicts in survivors, across all age groups.[1] Some of the factors that determine the extent and type of disturbance include the age at which the child experienced the abuse, the relationship of the perpetrator to the child, the frequency of the abuse, and the specific physical sexual acts. Not uncommonly, the perpetrator had previously been a trusted and caring relation in the child's life—someone the child would believe would treat them with kindness. Partly out of trust, out of a wish to please, out of unmet emotional needs for love and affection, and out of naïveté and confusion, the child willingly consents to abusive acts and may initially feel quite special, even adored.

However, these feelings quickly give way to deeply painful, confusing, and contradictory feelings and extensive damage to the emerging self and self-esteem. The feelings are so intense and overwhelming that they are frequently repressed and become unconscious, maybe even remembered only years later during the course of psychotherapy. They may become a principal reason for entering therapy as a result of a chronic pattern of disturbed relationships with lovers and with the self. They may also lead to higher rates of suicide.[2]

♪ **Session Soundtrack** ♪

The Carrie Underwood song "Blown Away" describes emotions related to childhood sexual abuse from the point of view of the victim. Carrie portrays her father as evil, praying that a coming tornado will blow her house down with her father trapped inside and condemned to a horrible death. The gathering storm clouds may be a metaphor for the rage she feels welling up inside of her as she remembers his sins committed in that house. But not even the torrential rains or fierce winds will be enough to wash or blow away the tear-soaked memories.

The theme of taking revenge against the perpetrator of child sexual abuse is further explored in the TV series *Ray Donovan*, which depicts the lingering effects of childhood sexual and physical trauma on adult sexual functioning, family dysfunction, and violence as a way of life.

Visit DrBruceKehr.com/music-9 for audio files
and further discussion of the soundtracks.

The feelings that emerge during the course of therapy with a patient who was sexually abused as a child may be so intense and frightening that they feel unmanageable. Therefore, a caring and empathetic bond with the therapist is crucial to working through the traumatic events without feeling overwhelmed, abandoned, or alone (yet again).

Powerful feelings of shame and humiliation are a cornerstone of the experience, and they mutilate the self-esteem of the child. The damaged self is then carried over into adulthood. The questions the survivor asks themselves often involve self-blame: *How could I have let this happen? What is wrong with me that I didn't stop it? What was it about me that caused it to happen in the first place? Why did I keep going back? I am damaged goods, and nobody will love me. I don't deserve to be loved.*

Humiliation Is a Powerful Emotion

Humiliation is one of the most painful and damaging of all human emotions.[3] It increases our emotional vulnerability and reduces our emotional reserve, which may lead to a downward spiral of hopelessness. When we are humiliated, particularly by someone we love or in the course of a major career or business setback, it can engender deep disappointment, hurt, anger, and even rage or suicidal behavior. If the humiliation occurs when we are also feeling generally despondent about life, the predisposition to depression, anger, and rage is even greater. Suffering deep humiliation in the absence of sufficient resilience and social support can be particularly dangerous.[4]

Brad's story illustrates two types of stress that can bring about feelings of humiliation and may characterize some of our important childhood relations (whether or not we suffered from trauma): **learned helplessness**, in which we repeatedly experience emotionally painful events that we are unable to predict or halt, and **social defeat stress,** in which we are repeatedly dominated or bullied in one or more important relationships. Each of these can also predispose us to depression and anxiety.

Another cornerstone is a sense of horror over what was done to them. The horror emerges from the ash heap of the memories of abuse. The victim will feel that horror over what was touched and where and how; the frightening realization that a previously loving and trustworthy person betrayed that trust; or feelings of murderous rage toward that person, which may include terrifying sadistic fantasies of revenge. A longing to be rescued and protected are also common.

The victim may feel both gratified and repulsed by being touched in private places by someone very special, which may fill them with guilt and shame. Wanting to destroy themselves—suicidal feelings, fantasies, and behaviors—is also part of the picture. Given how frightening the memories may be and the magnitude of the feelings engendered, the therapeutic alliance is often strained during the course of working with survivors of childhood sexual abuse.

Acting out to avoid these feelings may cause missed sessions, premature cessation of therapy, and emotionally painful sessions filled with sobbing and rageful shouting on the part of the patient. The corresponding feelings in the therapist may include sadness, wanting to hold and rescue and love the patient, and intense fury toward the perpetrator as the therapist empathizes with the memories and feelings of their patient as they emerge into conscious awareness.

The work is long and painstaking but immensely rewarding, because it enables the patient to begin to trust another human being, perhaps for the very first time. It opens them up to the possibility of loving and being loved, and it assists them in making sense of and recovering from all of the confusing feelings and memories that emerge during the course of the therapy.

Brad's Story

It is now time to bring home all of the lessons that we have learned about psychotherapy to this point. The role of a caring and empathetic therapist is crucial in a case like Brad's in providing a safe base, where you can feel emotionally safe, heal, and become whole. Please recall that, in our first session together, I characterized the unconscious as a vast swamp filled with repressed memories, feelings, demons, and our darkest thoughts. All of which serve to tangle up our heart. I spoke of how ridding ourselves of the demons in our hearts can be a terrifying process and that we keep them under wraps for good reason; to reawaken them may overwhelm and threaten to crush our sense of self. Brad's story will take us even deeper into the unconscious mind and, in some respects, will be the most powerful illustration so far of how therapy can put an end to feeling lost, hopeless, and alone.

I've purposely structured this story in great detail to authentically represent Brad's therapy. You may find it long and frustrating, and at times chaotic, but please be patient; this is the nature of healing deep emotional wounds. For someone who has survived childhood sexual abuse, and who now wishes to transcend it, the reality is that therapy unfolds slowly and painfully, but healing is possible with persistence, patience, and difficult but rewarding work with your therapist.

Brad was in his midfifties when he entered intensive therapy following the death of his mother. He had been in therapy earlier in his life, after his father died, and he had found the experience quite helpful. As a result, he was able to more rapidly develop a therapeutic alliance with me and more quickly open up about issues that were deeply painful to him than would someone who is entering therapy for the very first time. (Should you decide to enter therapy yourself, please give yourself plenty of time to develop confidence and trust in the therapist and the therapeutic process itself, which will enable you to explore issues like the ones Brad revealed from the beginning.)

Although Brad had been estranged from his mother for years, he had reconciled with her several months earlier. However, when she had become terminally ill, he was somehow unable to bring himself to visit her and was unwilling to speak with her by telephone in the weeks before her death. He felt puzzled and guilty about this inability to connect with her as she lay dying. Confused at his emotional paralysis and how he could have acted so callously toward his own mother, he asked for my help in making sense of it.

It was clear to me in our first session that this highly conscientious family man was suffering from feelings of guilt and shame over his avoidant behavior, and so I said, "Brad, you feel so guilty and ashamed of yourself for not having comforted your mother when she was lying on her deathbed, but there must be some unconscious reasons. Rather than berating yourself, let's try to understand them. Do you recall how you were feeling as you thought about calling or visiting with her?"

"At those moments," Brad said, "I felt panic, a sense of dread, and anger. But I don't know *why*. I was paralyzed with fear, but it made no sense to me, which just made me feel worse inside."

As an action-oriented man who prided himself in quickly addressing and solving problems, Brad's uncertainty and inability to find a plausible explanation for his behavior had filled him with deep frustration.

Remembering my own sense of impatience in my personal psychoanalysis—wanting to get to the bottom of my issues and work through them as soon as possible, to get off that couch quickly, because I felt so uncomfortable—I responded, "Brad, as you learned in your prior therapy, unconscious feelings and memories cannot be forced into consciousness. If we are patient and persistent, when you feel safe enough to tolerate them, these memories and feelings will emerge for us to explore and understand."

During his first session, Brad also divulged that he had begun angrily attacking those he cared about most. "And I've begun having nightmares about being a young boy attacked by a strange man. I used to have the same dream when I was a kid. I'd wake up screaming."

When he asked me what these nightmares might represent, I said, "We don't know for sure, but perhaps a very painful and traumatizing event is locked away in your unconscious mind, threatening to become conscious. Is it possible that you were physically or sexually abused as a child?"

"I don't know. I was afraid of my father, but I don't remember him ever being physically abusive. I don't remember any sexual abuse either—actual or threatened."

Once again, Brad felt frustrated that he couldn't fathom what might have triggered the nightmares to return after so many years.

"Brad, it's likely that the nightmares represent something deeply traumatic that you once experienced. There is no way to rush your recollection of what was done to you. Just keep talking about whatever comes into your mind, without censoring feelings or thoughts, regardless of how humiliating or threatening they may be. This includes bringing up any feelings or fantasies about me that you may develop. It is really important that you bring up these transference feelings,[5] which are normal and expected. If you withhold them out of shame or embarrassment, your therapy may not progress."

Talking with Brad throughout his early sessions allowed me to gain valuable insight into his world and to enter it as fully as possible. To be of most help to him—or, for that matter, to anyone I treat in a psychoanalytic psychotherapy—I need to join them where they live, deep inside their inner world, while simultaneously and seam-lessly moving between my own inner world (throughout my entire lifespan), my years of training and experience, and other patient stories and the lessons that I learned from them. This is all in the service of understanding and healing. The more you share with your therapist, the more we can help.

Brad enjoyed his profession as a highly sought-after, award-winning physician. He was held in high regard by his peers in the community and ran a prestigious concierge internal medicine prac-tice where his patients were quite fond of him. Nonetheless, Brad felt far less accomplished at home in his relationship with his wife, Melinda, and their two sons. He also suffered from a number of sexual inhibitions, which he felt ashamed about.

As he shared these details in our early sessions, I continued to reassure him. "Brad, if and when you are ready to explore your sexu-ality, we can do so. There is no need to feel pressured." Inside, I wondered again whether the inhibitions he alluded to related to his having been sexually abused as a child.

Even if my instincts were accurate, our therapeutic alliance would strengthen if I was patient with Brad and didn't push him. That was the best way to help him experience me as someone he could feel emotionally safe with. His therapy needed to unfold at its own pace; otherwise, he might feel intruded on or violated. Any hint of my forcing a premature result would negate the emerging feelings of emotional safety and trust that he was developing toward me. A doctor's urge to heal a patient—to get to the bottom of what's wrong and lessen their pain—needs to be tempered by a great respect for mechanisms that defend against threatening unconscious memories and feelings.

At this early phase of Brad's therapy, based on what he had dis-closed so far, my initial impression was that Brad was likely suffer-ing from midlife issues around facing and accepting that he was growing older, that the horizon ahead was diminishing and increasingly experienced as finite. However, this life-stage formulation didn't explain his nightmares or his phobic avoidance of his dying mother. Something was missing in Brad's story and in my formulation. As it turned out, it was something far more disturbing than either of us could have possibly imagined.

Over the next several months, Brad began to more deeply trust me. We began to peel back the layers of his unconscious memories and feelings. We grew to like each other and developed a deeper affection toward one another, and my patient, persistent, unhurried, nonjudgmental, and empathetic approach with him enabled Brad to feel safe. This allowed him to dig ever more deeply into his memories and feelings and, eventually, to bring the disturbing demons inside of him to light.

As we explored Brad's relationship with his mother, he recalled how angry he had felt toward her, given how uninvolved—even hurtful—she had been as the grandmother of his two sons. For example, she had a habit of bringing up sad or dreadful world events during celebrations such as her grandsons' birthdays or school awards ceremonies. Brad believed that his anger toward her explained why he couldn't bring himself to visit her on her deathbed.

Repeated empathic connections will enable a patient to go ever deeper, and so I shared my reaction: "Brad, how thoughtless of her to poison those events, to diminish the pure joy your family would experience during those precious moments. From what you are describing, at other times, your mother also disrespected you and your wife by disparaging your sons' behavior and blaming your style of parenting them."

He nodded in agreement and went on. "Her behavior infuriated me. And the way she treated them made my children feel uncomfortable around her and had hurt their feelings. Over the years, she also refused to visit us, or she'd stay only briefly, leaving as soon as she could. Instead, she'd hold court at her place. And she'd act strangely, alternately insulting and depressing us.

"She was a chronic depressive; nothing would ever make her happy. As long as I can remember, she popped painkillers, and went to rehab several times. I think she was also on barbiturates when I was a kid; she claimed that she needed to take them—a lot of them—to treat her frequent migraines."

Even though Brad's mother had been left a sizeable estate following the death of his father, she was living beyond her means, and Brad had been concerned that she would run out of money and then turn to him for financial support, which would add substantial strain to his relationship with Melinda.

"Melinda already hates my mother, and the prospect of telling Melinda that we'll have to financially support my mother really scares me."

As you learned in our earlier sessions, we therapists use countertransference to more deeply understand, emotionally resonate with, and enter our patient's world so they feel less alone. Recalling how I felt in my own childhood, raised by a mother who was emotionally unavailable and who also suffered from chronic depression, I felt a deep compassion for Brad.

I said, "Brad, as a boy, you longed for your mother to be loving, strong, and protective of you and attuned to your needs and feelings. But her depression and self-absorption rendered her emotionally unavailable. You probably felt quite alone. Can you recall how you felt toward her in those years?" This comment helped him to open up even more.

Peeling back the layers is a delicate process, with my questions serving as a surgical instrument, thoughtfully and meticulously and slowly uncovering and revealing under the best of circumstances. Unfortunately, at times, a patient may experience these questions as a blunt instrument. Despite all of the thought and care behind them, deep wounds may be suddenly and forcefully exposed.

At first, and somewhat paradoxically, Brad reported that "as a young boy, despite all her obvious problems, I idealized—even revered—my mother. I'm not sure why, and with how her behavior made me feel later, I find it surprising. But I remember thinking she was beautiful and that she comforted me when I was scared or sick with her soft touch and tender voice. She made me feel very special, like the most special person in her entire life."

During this exploratory phase, I did my best to be as empathetic as possible, perhaps even more so than usual, because I sensed that something more insidious and disturbing was at play within his unconscious mind, that something really bad lurked beneath his idealization of her. My instincts told me that we were merely scratching the surface, that something more sinister was about to emerge—and, eventually, it did.

We were now six months into Brad's therapy, and he had deeply internalized me as someone who really cared about understanding him in a way that no one ever had before. He had repeatedly experienced me as someone who was willing to enter his world alongside him, to work hard to shed light on some dark recesses, and to reliably and faithfully be there for him.

Suddenly, something shifted, and Brad expressed an inexplicable desire to drop out of therapy but couldn't explain why. Given our strong therapeutic relationship, he resisted these impulses and began to explore the underlying feelings. I supported this by explaining to him the healing effects of *abreaction* by saying, "Brad, what you are experiencing is not at all uncommon when disturbing memories and feelings are about to break through into consciousness. This can provoke anxiety, can even be quite frightening, but it will become part of the process of healing as the experiences emerge and we make sense of them with our adult eyes." (Recall our definition of *memory reconsolidation* in session 2.)

During his previous experience in psychotherapy, Brad had experienced intense feelings of anger and sadness about his relationship with his father but had ultimately come to terms with his unmet childhood need for an emotionally close and loving relationship. He was able to reconcile this with his father's tremendous devotion to teaching Brad about so many aspects of life—Saturdays spent working on cars together, building things, fixing appliances, and experimenting with a chemistry set. Brad's childhood dreams were ultimately fulfilled by the wonderfully positive and loving relationship that they developed in the last five years of his father's life. His father had undergone a personal transformation in his own therapy, becoming more approachable and loving.

Brad recognized that these conscious feelings certainly couldn't explain his strong desire to run away from me and our work together. He hadn't felt like abandoning his prior therapy and therefore began to feel that his disturbance with his mother was somehow of a different order of emotional magnitude. But why, and how?

Further clues began to unfold.

"In my previous therapy," he said, "I became aware of intense anger toward my mother. I attributed it to memories of her not protecting me from my father's scary outbursts and to her frequently taking to bed with headaches, backaches, or depression instead of facing life, taking care of her children, and confronting her husband.

"But there's something different this time. I'm frightened, but I can't explain why. I thought I had already dealt with this stuff, with my hatred of my mother. In here with you, I am feeling more and more like what I felt when I thought about visiting her on her deathbed."

"Brad, you are growing more and more frightened as certain unconscious memories threaten to become conscious, and you have described feeling more alone in the world and in our sessions here. Perhaps you also felt this way as a boy.

"To enable me to provide you more emotional support, would you be willing to come in and see me twice a week, at least for the time being? This may help you feel more emotionally held in here. You are demonstrating great courage in facing whatever is about to emerge, and I very much admire you for that. Whatever it is, this time around, you don't need to face it by yourself. You are no longer alone. I am here to listen, understand, and help."

Here, I was trying to reinforce my role as a healing companion, to let him know that I would not abandon him, and to hopefully give him explicit permission to explore his fears of abandonment in the context of revealing something he believed to be quite terrible. To go still deeper, it was essential that Brad come to trust me fully and completely.

Although Brad appreciated my comments, he was also afraid that I would abandon him once I learned whatever it was that he was going to reveal, which he felt extremely ashamed about.

"But I can't fathom what happened to make me feel this way," he said. "They're feelings without corresponding memories. I think my fears of you abandoning me somehow relate to my father; he was unable or unwilling to be there for me emotionally when I needed him. But where are my intense feelings of shame coming from?"

As trust in the therapist continues to develop and deepen over time, so does a patient's confidence in going ever deeper into what may be more and more disturbing memories. We were now nine months into Brad's therapy, and there was finally a huge breakthrough.

"It's finally come back to me," Brad said. "I must have been about four. I saw my mother undressing in her bedroom closet. She invited me in. I was curious, and because I adored her and was a good boy who did what she asked, I went in.

"Once I was inside the closet, she said, 'It's okay, Brad. Don't be afraid.'

"And then she had me place my hand on her vagina. She started explaining that this was where babies came from and that it was okay for me to touch her there and move my hand around."

As Brad's memories came out, he began sobbing. "Why would my mother do such a thing to me? I feel so ashamed that I would have done this with her."

I empathized: "Brad, you were just a small boy and had no knowledge that what she was doing was wrong. You had trusted her and relied on her to care for you and do what was right. She was your mother; you had unconditional love for her. You simply obeyed her wishes, as any young child would do."

My remarks brought him some temporary relief, but for the time being, further exploration of his mother's molestation felt like too much to bear, so Brad changed the subject and began discussing aspects of his career for a few sessions. I fully supported this. In the therapy of someone who has survived childhood sexual abuse, they should never be pushed into revealing further or faster; this could serve to worsen the trauma and would be what we call an *empathic failure*. You should feel that you have all of the time in the world to share with your therapist. It offers some semblance of control among powerful and uncontrollable feelings.

And then, he felt frightened again and wanted to run from a session.

"This time," he said, "I think it has to do with my intense rage toward my mother. It's overwhelming me in a way that feels unbearable, massive, bottomless, endless. It feels hopeless—like I might never get over these feelings. It feels like my anger toward her is just too vast."

And for the first time, Brad said something that chilled me to the bone, that he would repeat from time to time in the months ahead:

"Maybe it would be better for everyone if I just went up to the roof of my office building and walked off the edge."

The building was twelve stories high.

He went on: "Don't worry; I have no plans to do so, it's just a feeling I get when my anger feels overwhelming and unbearable."

I found little comfort in his efforts to reassure me.

Recalling this phase of my own personal psychoanalysis and how frightened and alone I felt at the time, I reassured and supported him by noting with a warm and caring voice, "Brad, you can talk with me about your anger and rage toward her at your own pace, a little bit at a time, and we will work through it together for as long as it takes."

Shortly thereafter Brad went away on vacation and experienced a flashback, triggered by seeing a beautiful blonde woman on a bicycle, at a distance, who reminded him of his mother when she was young. He suddenly had extremely vivid memories of her from even earlier in his childhood that felt real in the present, as if he were catapulted back there.

In our first session after he returned, Brad was a two- or three-year-old boy in his mind: "I just had a vivid flash. I'm crawling over my mother's body, playing with her breasts and her vagina, and feeling happy. There's nothing sexual or disturbing about it; it feels like I'm just a little boy playing."

Nonetheless, his good feelings were short-lived. They gave way to more horrifying feelings as memories began to surface of what we both came to know as *The Room*.

From deep inside Brad's unconscious mind, a memory surfaced. "I remember playing on the floor of the living room with my brother when I was about five years old. My dad was away on a business trip, and my mother was upstairs. A strange man approached the front door, began knocking, and asked to be let in.

"Something about him was scary, and I shouted to my mother

that a stranger was at the door and that I felt scared. My dad always told me that I should never let a stranger into the house, and I just wanted the man to go away.

"My mother peered down the stairway from the second floor and told me she knew the man; it was fine to let him in. I obeyed, but I felt a sense of dread. Something about the man was not right.

"The strange man walked into the house, his eyes darting around the room where my younger brother and I were playing. Then, my mother came down the stairs, looking very beautiful, with a big smile on her face. She greeted the scary man warmly, took his hand, and led him upstairs, telling me, 'Go play with your brother. Mommy will be busy for a while.' Not long afterward, I heard some odd noises coming from my parents' bedroom, which sounded like my mother was moaning and in pain."

The noises alarmed Brad, so he walked upstairs timidly. He noticed that the door to his parents' bedroom—The Room—was ajar. Peaking inside, he saw his mother with a strange man moving on top of her.

"It looked like he was hurting her. At that moment, my mother noticed me and said, 'Brad what are you doing? I told you to stay downstairs and play!' The man also looked at me in a menacing way, and I ran. I hid in the basement, in a dark corner, and started crying."

He felt so bewildered and scared, and when his mother came down in her bathrobe, quietly weeping and frightened, to try to console him, he just kept on crying and told her to go away.

"I pleaded with her to make the bad man go away. I felt hurt and confused. She tried to comfort me and cajoled me to come upstairs. When I finally gave in and climbed the stairs, the bad man was still there, which scared me even more. He made me sit down at the kitchen table across from him.

"He shook his finger at me and said angrily, 'You need to promise your mother and me that you will never tell your father about any-thing you saw here today. Promise us now!'

"I didn't want to lie to my father, who always told me to tell the truth, but I was scared of this menacing man and of my mother's crying, so I agreed. Then the man left. Later, my mother came to me and implored me not to tell my father, because the strange man might come back and hurt us if I revealed this secret."

Brad recalled that she seemed scared of the man as well. As he and I explored this event, Brad came to feel that the man was probably supplying his mother with the drugs she used to treat her "migraines" and that this was the man who attacked him in his nightmares.

A few months after this incident, Brad recalled, he came home early from school one afternoon. "As I entered the house, I heard the same groaning noises coming from my parents' bedroom. I immediately felt afraid but was curious and decided to investigate.

"When I went upstairs and peaked into the room, I saw my mother with a different man this time. Something about this man seemed friendly and familiar, not scary like the first man." Brad recognized him as the father of a little girl who lived up the street. He liked the little girl a lot, and they would sometimes hold hands and walk to school together.

Brad's mother invited him into the room, and into the bed with her and her lover. Being the dutiful son, Brad obeyed her, taking in the smells of cigarette smoke and liquor.

"I felt special for being invited in and was filled with anticipation and excitement, believing that we were all about to play some special games. I thought the bed would be kind of like a sandbox and that we would all play together. I would be taught some new games—the ones that grownups played with no clothes on. It made me feel very important.

"My mother and the man were laughing and seemed so happy, so

211

I felt happy too as I entered the bed to join them. My mother then asked me to touch her vagina, to place my face down there, and then to touch the man's penis, which was quite erect, and to put my lips around it. I obeyed. . . . She was my mother after all! . . .

"My happy feelings rapidly evaporated. My mother and the man continued laughing, and then they each touched my erect penis and commented on how small it was and laughed even more. Then, feeling sad and bewildered, I started to cry. I wanted to disappear into the bed sheets, to run from The Room, to be anywhere but where I was at that moment."

He recalled feeling deeply tortured—in immense emotional pain—and feeling that he was going to break into a million pieces. He felt like he had died.

In the months that followed this revelation, Brad would return to these feelings, describing them at various times as "the murder of my Self" or saying that "my mother murdered my very soul."[6] Brad felt a deep shame and abject humiliation over what transpired in The Room, feelings that we would return to time and again during the course of his therapy.

Over the next two years, Brad and I explored the enormity of The Room and its profound effects on his developing sense of self and on his psychosexual development. We faced the immense task of helping him come to terms with what had happened and with how he felt about it. My emotional support, compassion, and empathetic responses during this phase of therapy became ever more important in enabling him to do the work.

We came to learn what Brad meant when he described "the death of [his] Self." His personality became fragmented into a number of Selves,[7] each of which would serve a purpose (that would become clearer over time) and would enable him to emotionally survive such a horrifying betrayal.

Brad began to experience a variety of feelings and fantasies about his mother and her lover.

"I'm furious that she would indiscriminately use me as a sexual object—a kind of sex toy. She had no concerns whatsoever for my feelings or what the experience would do to me. I want to kill both of them."

Brad had a number of violent, sadistic fantasies about how he would have done so. He spoke of urges to burn down or blow up his childhood home, killing everyone within it. The fantasies, which Brad experienced at times as intense feelings or impulses to take action, were so gruesome that they terrified him; he didn't believe himself to be evil, to be capable of even imagining such horrors, let alone carrying them out.

These murderous feelings commonly emerge during the course of therapy with survivors of childhood sexual abuse and are quite frightening for the patient. They are completely understandable, given the horror of what was done to them. Reassuring the patient that these feelings can be explored, tolerated, and slowly worked through over an extended time is crucial to their progress. In Brad's case, they helped explain why he had panicked over the thought of visiting his dying mother; underneath those feelings of panic were intense, unconscious impulses to murder her.

Brad once said to me, "In The Room, my mother gave birth to two new boys—Monster Boy and Fake Boy—and she killed off Sweet Boy." We began to explore each of these new Selves inside of Brad and their significance in enabling him to survive his childhood.

The Monster Boy represented all the more horrifying aspects inside of him. Monster Boy had been hidden away in Brad's unconscious mind for all of these years—defended against, repressed, and dissociated from conscious awareness as a powerful and overwhelmingly frightening Self.[8]

♪ **Session Soundtrack** ♪

As Brad began to reveal Monster Boy's attributes, I thought of that haunting song "Tornado," by Jonsi, the guitarist and vocalist for the Icelandic post-rock band Sigur Rós. The lyrics speak of something inside that is disguised yet known. It grows and roars like a tornado and will destroy everything. It will erupt like a volcano and kill everything in its path. The singer, struggling with the gloom of depression, will learn to know about this thing inside of him and wonders if he will ever be allowed to be free—or even to simply be. When I shared this song with Brad, it resonated with him and with his Monster Boy. It helped his Monster Boy feel less alone inside him.

Visit DrBruceKehr.com/music-10 for audio files
and further discussion of the soundtracks.

As these memories came back to him, I shared with him the following over the course of a number of sessions: "Brad, the sadistic and violent feelings you have toward your mother and her lover are completely understandable. The two of them violated you in so many profoundly horrible ways. Your mother destroyed your trust in her. She abandoned you and shattered your love for her. She and her lover desecrated your sexual development and your very self as a sweet and caring young boy. They stole your childhood, and she devastated your heart. And then they both humiliated you further by laughing at you.

"As a result, you became enraged at them and wanted to take revenge. Monster Boy came about to protect and defend you, to ensure that you would never be violated again by your mother or anyone else. Your violent feelings and fantasies of taking revenge were completely normal, even expectable under the circumstances, and have to do with trying to protect yourself, to keep you safe from any future harm. And yet, because Monster Boy threatened your mother's very existence and because you needed her so much and couldn't bear the thought of killing her, you had to immediately bury him deep inside your unconscious."

At this point, I felt that it might be helpful to Brad if I introduced the idea that none of what happened was his responsibility and that it was the responsibility of the adults in his life to protect him. I did this by saying, "If I had been there, I would have protected you, and your mother would never be able to do such a thing again. I would have ensured that both she and her lover would face criminal charges and that they would be imprisoned for committing such terrible acts against you."

Not uncommonly, Brad would weep as I empathized with his feelings, and then he would feel enraged that the sweet and caring young boy and the peaceful, emotionally comforting life he'd been living had been destroyed, never to return. Sweet Boy had died, and in his place was the sadistic, violent, and tortured Monster Boy, who he had hidden from himself all of these years. Monster Boy was such a terrifying Self that Brad had split him off into his unconscious, along with the memories of his repeated sexual abuse (this is known as *dissociative amnesia*).[9]

At times in our sessions, when the violent and sexually sadistic Monster Boy Brad came out, Brad would first feel enraged, and then feel physically paralyzed, as if the paralysis would somehow protect his mother from his wishes to assault her. At other times, he would describe feeling strangely dissociated from the room, himself, and me. The paralysis and dissociation were defenses against the strength of his fury, which felt so scary and shameful to him.

At the same time Monster Boy was created, another "boy" had been formed out of the ashes of his prior life—Fake Boy. Fake Boy focused almost all of his energies on pleasing his mother and father and never getting angry, speaking up, or rocking the boat. "It was like I became one of those performing monkeys—you know, the ones that bang the cymbals to receive favors." In some respects, this furthered Brad's feelings of humiliation. Fake Boy believed that if he could just survive and work incredibly hard in school, he could escape his terrible childhood and become a powerful adult.

Brad noted, "I decided that I would become powerful so that nobody could ever fuck with me again!" And so he became a straight-A student who ran away from the present by living in the future. He became obsessed with space and time travel and imagined a future where he would be invincible—where nobody could ever hurt him again.

"I feel ripped off and cheated," he said. "I'm furious that the mother I loved and trusted subjected me to these atrocities. She devastated my heart."

In therapy, Brad would sometimes shout and scream out, and, at other times, he would sob uncontrollably, and say, "I have a rent in my soul. It feels like a searing pain, unimaginably painful, tearing my soul in two. Words can't begin to describe it. I feel that if I didn't have that pain I would come apart in a million pieces. Underneath that pain is nothingness. Without it, nothing would be left of me."

I felt so helpless and enraged about what his mother had put him through and felt such immense fury toward her that I had to be aware of and manage my own feelings, to use them in the service of compassion and empathy and not express them in a way that would make Brad feel unsafe with me.

Any caring therapist will experience these intense countertransference feelings from time to time while working with a patient who has been traumatized. When brought into conscious awareness, the feelings help the therapist become and remain a steadfast and caring companion, and as such, they can be used to heal the aloneness felt by the patient. Recall that, in an earlier session, I spoke of how helping a patient is both an honor and a privilege—a calling. With Brad, I often felt this way.

Another dilemma emerged for Brad, since both his mother and her former lover had already died.

"I'll never be able to confront them, to take revenge for what they did."

At one point, he became furious with me, shouting, "What good is your compassion and empathy! It is useless! I want to take action and exact revenge by destroying both of them, but we sit here doing nothing. I want to take my father's guns and shoot them both in the head! Shoot that fucking cunt of a mother! I want to shoot that drug dealer guy, too! That fucking asshole that invaded our home and scared the shit out of me! This therapy is worthless, and you are useless to me!"

His transference reaction was completely understandable, given his deep longing to have been protected and defended by a responsible adult and, absent that, his strong urges to exact revenge against his abusers, to try to restore his honor and self-respect, and to achieve some modicum of justice. Brad was also furious that Monster Boy existed at all, that this twisted, rage-filled, sexually sadistic part of himself would never go away.

Uncertain whether it would be of any help, I empathized with him by saying, "Brad, it is horribly unfair that there is no justice to be found in any of this, given that they are all dead. You cannot confront them, have them arrested, or make them pay for what they did. The atrocities they committed on your body and your Self, as a sweet and loving boy who entered that room filled with curiosity and innocence, should have resulted in their being brought to justice and severely punished. That punishment will never be meted out, and for that matter, no amount of punishment would ever compensate you for what they did. My efforts to console you will not make up for it either.

"Perhaps there is a small measure of comfort to be found in knowing that you developed the strength to survive what she did to you, build a loving family, and establish a career as an esteemed physician healing thousands of patients. There is a richness to your life that your mother never experienced."

Brad appreciated my remarks, wept, and said, "At age five, I knew that I had to get the hell out of there. I knew that I was a smart little boy and that, if I worked hard in school and believed in myself, I could survive and create a wonderful life in the future. This fantasy sustained me. It was preferable to killing her, killing my family, or killing myself. And as you point out, I *have* been successful in creating a wonderful life—a life I could only dream of when I was a child. Dreaming of that future life kept me alive."

Over time, through my repeated efforts to connect, support, explain, and clarify what Brad lived through and experienced in The Room and its aftermath, and his courage to repeatedly face what was done to him and grieve, he began to develop a series of memory reconsolidations. Recall that *memory reconsolidation*[10] is the process that enables previously consolidated, emotionally traumatic memories to be reconsolidated, or overwritten, such that new learning renders them less traumatic. As a result of Brad's abreactive experiences and the caring and empathy I provided, the traumatic events were recast in a new cognitive framework and viewed without distortion through our adult eyes, enabling Brad to begin to let go of the trauma.

Over several months, Brad's fury began to subside.

"Maybe I've taken revenge against my mother after all, without even knowing it," he said, and this realization began to make him feel a little better.

"I imagine her lying in her deathbed, all alone, aware that I was refusing to visit, and I hope that, as she lay there reviewing her life, she was filled with shame and remorse over what she did to me. I hope she realized I was paying her back." This picture brought him a small measure of solace.

Brad came to realize that his mother had repeatedly overstimulated him sexually at other times as well—coming into his bedroom in the middle of the night, reaching under the covers, and touching his penis while softly and sweetly cooing to him. Horrified, and filled with intense shame that he had become sexually stimulated, he cried out to me, "Is there no end to this depravity?! What a horrible person I must be! How is it possible that I became sexually excited when she touched me down there? What kind of sick and distorted child would permit this to happen?!"

He would weep again when discussing these events. Feeling intense shame, Brad sobbed over how he had sexually stimulated his mother: "She made me touch her down there, and I remember now that it gave her pleasure! What a disgusting, horrible person I am! How can I ever allow the people I love the most in this world to look me in the eye—my children, my wife, you—when all they will see is someone who committed such disgusting behaviors? You see, no matter how much you try to explain this away as my being an innocent boy who didn't know any better, there is no taking it back. Ever. I can never make up for what I did!" At times like these he would once again fantasize about walking off that rooftop.

Softly and gently, I helped Brad explore this, and together, we came to understand that he would never have initiated any of these sexual experiences with her on his own and that his sexual excitement was a natural physiologic response.

On one occasion, he erupted and shouted, "But why did I allow her to keep coming back?! Why didn't I tell her to stop? Or hide a knife under the covers and stab her to death the next time she came in? That would have put an end to it!"

Brad came to understand that he would have done anything to experience his mother's love, that he had such a deep need to feel loved and special, and that none of what he permitted to be done to him had anything to do with sex. Any young child has a profound need to be loved by their mother.[11]

"I adored her; she was so beautiful," he said. "I fully and completely trusted her to take care of and protect me. And given her frequent crying spells and how many times she said she was unhappy, I would have done anything to make her smile, to make her happy." He had idealized her, and in return, she idealized him, all of which was quite intoxicating for Brad and impossible to resist.

Over time, Brad's Monster Boy was able to come out of hiding, to feel less alone, and to be understood by both of us. In our therapy sessions, we would engage in discussions with Monster Boy, and I would encourage him to speak out and let us hear from him directly about what he thought and felt.

Monster Boy told us, "I never really wanted to hurt anyone unless they threatened me or Fake Boy with some form of abuse. I merely wanted to end my loneliness, to feel safe, and to be loved."

We continued to explore Brad's memories of Fake Boy, Sweet Boy, and Monster Boy. We brought each of these Selves to life in our sessions to more fully understand their characteristics. I encouraged Brad to allow each of the three Selves to begin communicating with one another. Through a process whereby each Self would talk to the others—Brad as Sweet Boy, who felt happy, trusting, and whole, with a normal sexual curiosity, prior to the traumatic events in The Room; Brad as Monster Boy, filled with mistrust and sadistic sexual, rageful, vengeful feelings and urges; and Brad as Fake Boy, who complied with his mother's and father's wishes to be able to survive into the future. My hope was that each of these Selves could eventually reconcile and become one unified Self within Brad.

During this phase of his therapy, my strategy was to enable Brad to begin to feel whole inside, through accepting aspects of himself that had previously been dissociated off into his unconscious. These parts of himself had shamed, humiliated, and horrified him. We spent much of our time together coming to understand Monster Boy, because he weighed so heavily on Brad's sense of self (contributing to Brad's occasional desire to kill himself just to kill off

Monster Boy), felt so abhorrent to him, and had been split off from his conscious awareness for decades. We both came to understand that Monster Boy had been created for a very good reason.

"Brad," I said, "Monster Boy was born out of your horror and sadness over having been abused and evolved as your protector, to ensure that you would never again be molested or taken advantage of by anyone. Monster Boy was hidden for decades, then demonized as he began to emerge in therapy, and now he has become humanized as a necessary defense against what had been done to you by your mother and her lovers. Monster Boy, like all of us, just wants to be loved and cared for by someone."

As Brad progressively integrated Monster Boy, Fake Boy, and Sweet Boy into one cohesive Self, a new phase in his therapy began, a phase characterized by his recognition of and grief over the many aftereffects of his mother's repeated molestation. In the process of becoming whole, Brad was now able to see the mutilating effects of the trauma on his relationship with his father, his sexuality, and his adult love relations and to mourn those losses.

He began to realize that deep feelings of shame had infected his life in a number of ways over the years. He described it as feeling "covered in shit, in my mother's filth because I stayed in The Room and performed shameful acts with her and her lovers." In a similar vein, at other times Brad would say, "I feel like I am filled with pus inside that needs to be drained; like there is a terrible sickness infecting my entire being."

Brad's feelings of shame permeated his social being as well. Although he was quite successful, he had always felt painfully shy and had difficulty looking others in the eye when speaking with them. Although he was an attractive man, he had felt ashamed of his appearance and disgusted by his physique.

Brad was furious over how his mother's reprehensible behavior had stolen what had been normal sexual curiosity. In its place, he had developed sexual inhibitions—and underneath, the sexually sadistic Monster Boy. The inhibitions came to be understood as a way to keep Monster Boy at bay, under wraps in Brad's unconscious mind. It had been just too emotionally threatening to allow Monster Boy to come out of the shadows until after Brad's mother had died.

Brad would often express anger toward me for not protecting him from his mother, then realize that his anger was misplaced. It was actually meant for his father, who failed to notice the changes in his son. Brad felt betrayed that his father didn't pick up on how his little buddy, his best friend, had withdrawn from him and didn't ask him what was wrong. Where was the emotional help and support that he so desperately needed? Why had his father failed to rescue him?

One time, Brad recalled, his mother ran away from home, with him in tow and without his father, to her parents' summer home. He awoke one night to his father fiercely pounding on the door, shouting and screaming to let him in. When Brad's mother opened the door, Brad hid under a table, afraid his father would violently assault her, possibly kill her. He thought that his father might have just discovered her affair, and he felt so sad for his father and even more furious at his mother for hurting his dad and destroying their family life.

In our therapy session, Brad wept. "I thought I could never tell my dad what had happened in The Room, because I was afraid that he would kill my mother and her lover." With great sadness, Brad recalled that around this time, "my father grew more emotionally distant, and I withdrew from him too. I was ashamed and felt like I had been messing around with my father's wife. I had also betrayed him by letting a dangerous stranger into the house and by concealing what I had seen them doing." Confronting these feelings was incredibly painful for Brad, yet he hung in there and would faithfully and reliably attend our sessions.

Barely concealing my own anger toward his father, I said, "Brad, your father should have noticed that you were changing, growing more distant from him, and he could have asked you what was happening. It was his responsibility as the adult to be attuned to what was going on—not yours. You were just a young boy. You were merely trying to make your mother happy in The Room, given how sad you had felt about her chronic unhappiness, and the horrible acts she committed on you drove you to withdraw. Your feelings of horror, sadness, guilt, and shame caused you to turn away from your dad, and it was his job to reach out to you."

I admired Brad's courage and would validate his feelings of sadness and rage. I pointed out many times that, with respect to his feelings of shame, he had been only a young boy, and a good boy who trusted his mother—who, of course, would have obeyed her.

Remembering how I felt as a young child and what it felt like being the father of two young girls and in the service of once again joining Brad where he was emotionally living at that very moment in our session, I said, "Brad any young boy needs a mother to fully trust, to take care of, and to protect him—to make him feel safe. This is the central role of any good mother. You must have felt terribly alone during those times, because you could not turn to your father either. Alone and abandoned, bereft, confused, you did not have a safe base where you could take all of the intense feelings you were having and talk about them. Because you did not feel emotionally safe with either parent, it must have been difficult to survive. Your situation was impossible. It is truly remarkable how you endured these events to become an accomplished and caring doctor, father, and husband."

As he continued to grieve, Brad's heart and soul inexorably began to heal. "At this point," he told me, "you're the only person on earth I've shared all of my memories and feelings with, and I feel a deep gratitude that I no longer have to feel all alone with them."

Our trusted relationship had become unshakeable, unbreakable. However, as much as he fervently wanted to and regardless of how hard he worked in therapy, it was impossible for Brad to blow away all of the horrible memories or to rid himself of Monster Boy. He felt tortured at times, wondering aloud (as in that Jonsi song) whether he would ever be free.

"Will I ever be allowed to just *be*?" he asked.

But as Brad faced the horrors of The Room and Monster Boy and as we worked together to make sense of it all within the framework of caring empathy, the power of those memories continued to diminish.

"I used to feel like a fraud," he said. "I lived so much of my life as Fake Boy; now I feel more authentic. I feel supported, even loved here, in therapy, and in other areas in my life like I never have before.

"I've rediscovered memories of my dog—my best friend and confidant when I was a kid—and of my grandparents, who were loving and supportive. The three of them saved my life. *You* saved my life as well. Thank you for truly being there for me during this painful journey, for not abandoning me. Your caring presence elicits feelings of love for you, which gives me the confidence and the emotional strength to press onward."

We were now three years into Brad's psychoanalytic psychotherapy. This illustrates a really important point: It can take a long time to develop those really deep bonds of trust that enable the work of abreaction and memory reconsolidation. This is why it is vital that, once you engage with a therapist who really understands you and who provides an emotionally safe place where you can reveal anything and everything, you stick with your therapy and see it through to full recovery.

Brad now felt safe enough with me to reveal with intense shame that "a part of me had actually wanted to be in The Room with my mother and her lover and wanted to have physical contact with them, to 'play' together." He had been filled with excitement, both emotional and sexual.

"These memories make me feel terrible," he said. "How is it possible that I could actually *want* to be sexually abused? Doesn't that mean I'm a despicable human being? That I'm evil? How could I *want* to be a part of something like that?" He was sickened and disgusted by his wishes.

I pointed out that he was exercising his adult judgment about what had happened. "You're looking back at it through adult eyes, Brad," I replied. "As a four- or five-year-old boy, you certainly would have no knowledge of the appropriateness of your participation in any of these experiences. You worshipped your mother and wanted to please her, irrespective of what she requested. And you had initially believed that The Room was a special place and that being invited into the bed was a sign of how special you must be. As a young boy, you believed that you would do very grown up things in that room just like your father and that your mother was going to introduce you to these things. They would help you become even more like your father, your best buddy, the man you cherished."

As Brad once again became that little boy, in the safety of my office, he felt all of the feelings that I just described but viewed them through the eyes of an adult, which allowed him to begin to forgive himself.

As I write this book, Brad and I continue to work together to untangle his heart and promote greater healing. He now understands why he could not visit his mother on her deathbed: It would likely have been a violent confrontation filled with intense urges to murder her, and he was unconsciously afraid that he would have been unable to control his rage and would have acted out his violent feelings. He was afraid that Monster Boy would have sprung to life to protect him by killing her. He has recovered memories of his mother abusing drugs, dating back to his early childhood, under the guise of using them to treat her migraine headaches, and he recollected how drugged she had been in The Room and at other times. Realizing that she was an addict has helped lessen the emotional pain he feels, at least a little bit. He can blame some of her pedophilic behavior on the barbiturates and opiates that she was taking, along with her episodic abuse of alcohol. Perhaps it was blackout behavior.[12]

Brad is now less frightened by our sessions and no longer feels the urge to run. His rage feels manageable, not boundless. He feels stronger both within the sessions and in his outside life. His suicidal feelings have dissipated. He has come to like Monster Boy, even love him, as a friend who is there to defend and protect him and his family in the event that anyone ever again threatened any of them. "If anybody tries to fuck with us, Monster Boy will kill them."

And Brad's relationship with himself and his loved ones has significantly improved. He has come to realize that his capacity to trust another human being had been deeply damaged by his mother's abusive behavior and, to a lesser extent, by his father's failure to rescue him from her clutches. With sadness, he became aware of how his deep mistrust had damaged his relationships with family and friends, who he had always kept an emotional distance from. He openly wept over this realization, recognizing how tormented he felt—on one hand, desperately wanting to give them his heart without holding back but, on the other, feeling terrified of being betrayed again.

"I still fear that a betrayal by someone I love will destroy me for good this time," he said. "Or it might unleash a Monster Boy who might be impossible to stop."

In general, Brad describes himself as "feeling lighter." He is allowing himself to more deeply trust in his loved ones and is less afraid to give his love to them and to let them more fully love him. Equally important, Brad feels sexually liberated and is much freer to explore his sexuality in the bedroom. Although much work remains to fully integrate the splintered aspects of his Self, we are both confident that he can achieve this as well.

Managing my own countertransference[13] feelings while listening to Brad has been challenging at times, although these feelings have also served to deepen my compassion and empathy for him. This is an example of why it is so important that a therapist has been on the other side of the couch, essential that they have completed their own intensive psychotherapy or psychoanalysis.

Begin to Heal

If you are a survivor of childhood sexual abuse, my heart goes out to you. You have traveled down a harder road than most. Not uncommonly, these experiences have profound effects on the development of one's Self. Below are some steps that you can take to begin to heal. However, a note of caution: Reach out to others for support as you embark on this exercise. Taking it on alone, without empathy, compassion, and ongoing emotional support from someone who loves you may not be advisable, because there may be powerful, profound, and disturbing emotions that will begin to surface from your unconscious mind. The support of a loved one will help you cope with them. Choose someone who is nonjudgmental and perhaps was abused themselves and has worked through these issues in their own therapy.

Once again, it would be useful to write your thoughts and feelings in your workbook.

Step 1: Begin to face what was done to you.

Wanting to run away from the memories and feelings is understandable, but healing only comes after you've faced your abuse and worked through it. This can be done through introspection and journaling (it can help sometimes just to write down your feelings, memories, and dreams). Who is a loved one you can turn to and share the feelings and memories that emerge? Approach them to see if they are willing to be emotionally available to you, over an extended time, as you start this journey. How confident do you feel about their ability to provide you continuing support?

Step 2: Recall how you were abused.

There are a number of important questions to begin to try to answer, yet it can be quite difficult to access unconscious memories of what happened. To the extent that you can remember, what was done to you? Who was the sexual predator? Was it one time or multiple times? How old were you? Write down as much as you can.

Step 3: Assess your mental state.

Do you suffer from some of the following symptoms of PTSD? If so, write them down in as much detail as possible.

- Recurring memories, flashbacks, or nightmares where you reexperience the traumatic event
- Panic attacks or increased emotional arousal
- Emotional numbing or distancing from people or places that remind you of the trauma
- Negative feelings about yourself and life

- Difficulty maintaining intimacy and emotional closeness
- A feeling that your future is foreshortened or hopeless
- Avoidance of places or memories associated with the traumatic event
- Irritability, angry outbursts, or aggressive behavior
- Always being on guard for danger
- Overwhelming feelings of guilt or shame
- Self-destructive behavior, such as drinking too much alcohol, abusing drugs, or driving too fast
- Trouble concentrating
- Difficulty sleeping
- Being easily startled or frightened

Step 4: How has the trauma affected you?

How might the sad and horrible traumatic experiences have affected your childhood and adult love relationships? How have they influenced your feelings about yourself, your self-esteem, and your self-respect?

Step 5: Was anyone else affected?

Are there others (siblings or close friends) who may have also been abused? Would you be willing to ask them what they remember? If so, write down what they report in as much detail as possible, gently probing for clarity, to get as many of your questions answered as possible.

Step 6: Get help.

Seek professional help. In addition to the support of loved ones and friends, there is hotline and online support available through RAINN (the Rape, Abuse, and Incest National Network),[14] support groups, therapists at community mental health centers, and psychiatrists and psychotherapists in private practice. If you are struggling with suicidal feelings, it is imperative that you enter treatment as soon as possible.

Step 7: Choose your therapist wisely.

You will want to work with someone who has deep experience in treating trauma victims. They should be trained in what is called **psychoanalytic/psychodynamic psychotherapy** or **prolonged exposure therapy** and should have been in intensive psychoanalytic therapy or psychoanalysis themselves.

The psychotherapy of survivors of childhood sexual abuse is facilitated by a safe, trusting, caring, and empathetic therapeutic alliance,[15] in the service of enabling regression back to childhood. You will repeatedly remember and face the traumatic experiences along with all of the attendant feelings about what was done to you and how it made (and makes) you feel about yourself.

Your therapist will serve as a kind of caring parent and friend, guide, mentor, and educator. If you have made the right choice, you should begin to feel a bond developing by the end of the first or second visit. You should feel that you like them and what they have to say. Over time, you will want to feel that they really, truly understand you; to feel completely emotionally safe with them; and to feel them at your side as a strong and resolute presence as you begin your difficult (and sometimes seemingly perilous) journey back into what was done to your physical and emotional self.

As was illustrated in Brad's story, it takes a great deal of courage to engage in longer-term psychotherapy and to repeatedly face what was done to you, the feelings engendered by the trauma, the resulting devastation of aspects of your Self, and confrontation of your abuser (whether in the therapy sessions or in real life). Enter therapy with optimism, and stick with it; the outcome can bring you a richer, far less disturbed relationship with yourself, those you love, and life itself.

* * *

This was perhaps our toughest session so far, wasn't it?

Hopefully, you now have a much deeper understanding of what happens to the human heart when a child has been sexually abused. If you have survived childhood sexual abuse, the story of Brad may give you hope that you too can recover. It may also help you begin to forgive yourself and may lighten your load just a little bit.

This concludes our sessions devoted to understanding what goes on in psychotherapy, and you hopefully now have a better idea of what you could expect in your own therapy. We have learned how patiently, persistently uncovering distressing memories and feelings, in the context of a warm, caring, and trusting therapeutic relationship, can bring about clarity and healing. You need to stick with it. Regardless of the origins of your tangled heart, you can now feel hopeful that the therapeutic process will facilitate untangling your life and becoming whole.

Our next session should prove to be enlightening and a lot less emotionally draining. I look forward to seeing you soon. Be well.

HEAL YOUR
FUTURE

SESSION TWELVE

How to Maintain Emotional Health and Self-Love

I open the door to the waiting room and you are sitting there quietly, lost in thought. Yet you look different today, compared with the first time I greeted you. You no longer appear distressed. Your face and body are more relaxed. When I welcome you into my office with a warm "hello," you look up at me, and a huge smile spreads across your face. Your eyes are far more alive than they once were; in fact, they sparkle. It is so gratifying for me as your doctor to see you feeling happier.

Today represents a milestone. It is our final session.

When you first came in to see me, you felt quite tangled up inside. Since that point, we have shared many moments together, and I deeply appreciate the confidence you have placed in me in revealing your heart and soul. I admire you for working so hard. I feel privileged to have helped you along the way and honored that you chose me to guide your journey.

You have learned new ways to think about yourself and the important relationships in your life and have thoughtfully answered my questions. I hope that you feel less burdened than before and have begun the process of healing your troubled heart and perhaps have imparted some of these lessons to others, to enable them to heal as well.

I hope this book has helped you realize you are not alone in your emotional pain and that there is hope for you to have a better future. I hope that you have learned valuable methods of introspection to untangle your life and end the patterns that sabotage your happiness, and that the process of psychotherapy is no longer as mysterious or frightening.

♪ Session Soundtrack ♪

The lyrics of that U2 song "Beautiful Day" portray what is possible when you resolve the issues that have tangled up your heart and end the patterns that have sabotaged your happiness. The words portray someone who is in a rut, out of luck, and going nowhere. They have no planned destination and may feel stuck. Perhaps this is how you felt about yourself and your life prior to our first session. The singer implores someone to touch him and take him somewhere else, to teach him because he knows it's not hopeless.

Isn't this the essence of what you have learned from our sessions? That you can move away from feeling hopelessly stuck and emotionally paralyzed through being touched and taken to another place by compassion and empathy, taught how to untangle your emotional life and love relations through introspection, medication, and psychotherapy, such that you will never become hopeless.

The song goes on to describe how beautiful the day can be.

This can be your destiny too, if you put into practice what you have learned from our time together. Don't let that beauty get away.

As a result of our sessions and all of your hard work, I fervently hope that you too have been touched, taught, and taken away to a place filled with less emotional pain and an appreciation of the beauty inside of you.

Visit DrBruceKehr.com/music-11 for audio files
and further discussion of the soundtracks.

You've Got a Plan

You have developed many insights, and this knowledge and understanding is but the beginning of the process, not the endpoint. The song "Atlas Hands," by Benjamin Francis Leftwich (DrBruceKehr.com/music-12), describes someone who has a plan, an atlas in their hands to guide them as they take the turns in the road ahead. They will chart their course by listening to the lessons that they have learned.

Through our work together, we have helped you create your own atlas: a map of your life's journey, from an earlier time leading up to the present day, and the means to chart a new course by providing a compass to assist you in navigating the journey that lies ahead. These lessons will help you to stay on course as you take new actions to further untangle your life. And to facilitate your staying on course, I have summarized all of our work together in **The Healing Companion Checklist** in the Appendix.

My friend, it is time for us to say goodbye. Allow me to take a moment to impart some final words of advice. I deeply care about the outcome of your life and would like to believe that our time together has eased some of your emotional distress and filled you with abundant hope for a happier future.

Listen to the lessons that you have learned and translate them into purposeful steps that will carry you forward. Please continue those important conversations within yourself and with those you love. Draw courage from the many patients whose stories I have shared with you.

Thank you for letting me touch your heart in so many places, and for allowing me to help you uncover your feelings, yearnings, strivings, wishes, and dreams.

One last note before we conclude: The work we began together is not quite finished. You will face new emotional challenges in the years ahead, and there will always be more to think about and understand. Please feel free to bring me along as a companion inside of you if it helps to ease your journey, and remember the sessions we shared and the lessons you have been taught. I have so much enjoyed our work together and wish you all the best. You are a very fine person and deserve all of the happiness that life can offer.

Disclaimer

The material and information provided within this book does not constitute medical advice, and the strategies and treatment modalities discussed in the sessions may not be applicable to you, your family members, or your friends. No part of the content of this book is intended by the author or publisher to be a substitute for professional medical advice, diagnosis, or treatment by a qualified mental healthcare professional. No physician–patient relationship, explicit or implied, exists between the publisher, author, and you, the reader. This book is not a substitute for a relationship between you, as a patient, and a qualified mental healthcare professional.

The patient stories contained within the book are illustrative of emotional issues faced by many of us as we go through life, and some of the themes presented are universal. Although lessons learned from the treatment of actual patients are included in the stories, the historical events and facts represented have been changed to protect the identities of any real patients and to protect their confidentiality. This includes, among other minor alterations, the names, ages, careers, the number and sex of their children, and the careers of the patients' parents. Consequently, all characters that appear in this work are fictitious. Any resemblance to real persons, living or dead, is purely coincidental.

The information included in each chapter or "session" is for illustrative and educational purposes only, to help you understand what your experience in a psychiatric session might be like. You should not consider such information to be medical advice that is in any way suitable to your circumstances, nor should you treat anything you read in this book as an alternative to medical advice that you receive from a doctor or other professional mental healthcare professional. Any use of the information in this book is at your discretion. Consult a qualified healthcare professional if you have any questions or concerns that relate to your own life situation. You should not delay obtaining medical or mental health advice, disregard medical or mental health advice, or discontinue medical or mental healthcare treatment because of any information you read in this book or any resources cited by the author in the book.

ALTHOUGH THE PUBLISHER AND THE AUTHOR HAVE USED THEIR BEST EFFORTS IN PREPARING THIS BOOK, THEY MAKE NO REPRESENTATIONS OR WARRANTIES WITH RESPECT TO THE ACCURACY OR COMPLETENESS OF THE CONTENT OF THIS BOOK. THE AUTHOR AND PUBLISHER SPECIFICALLY DISCLAIM ANY AND ALL LIABILITY ARISING DIRECTLY OR INDIRECTLY FROM THE USE BY ANY PERSON OF ANY INFORMATION CONTAINED IN THIS BOOK. THE DISCUSSIONS AND STRATEGIES CONTAINED IN THIS BOOK MAY NOT BE SUITABLE FOR YOUR PARTICULAR LIFE SITUATION. YOU SHOULD CONSULT A QUALIFIED MENTAL HEALTHCARE PROFESSIONAL FOR ANSWERS TO ANY QUESTIONS ABOUT THE APPLICABILITY TO YOU OF ANYTHING YOU MAY READ IN THIS BOOK OR IF YOU ARE UNSURE ABOUT HOW TO COPE EFFECTIVELY WITH YOUR THOUGHTS OR FEELINGS OR ANY OTHER ASPECT OF YOUR PERSONAL LIFE EXPERIENCE.

Acknowledgments

Deepest gratitude to each of my thirteen manuscript reviewers, whose (at times) brutal candor added immensely to the quality of this book. They are **Sue Clement, Jill Flax, Phil Gross, Lisa Kehr, Melanie Kehr, James MacIntyre III, Jeff MacIntyre, Ruby L. MacIntyre, Dr. Francis Mas, Dr. Arnold Meshkov, Dr. Robert Post, Elizabeth Riggins,** and **Terry Vinston.**

Drs. Avery Weisman, Bill Granatir, and **Doug Chavis,** psychoanalysts with whom I consulted during residency training and following the deaths of my father and mother, respectively, whose kindness, empathy, and insights have enabled me to deeply love another human being, compassionately help thousands of patients, and find the courage to write this book. And Doug, thank you for enabling me to "become whole" myself.

Psychoanalyst **Dr. David Eden** (my father-in-law), who taught me to "never underestimate the power of simply listening to your patient. You may be the first person in their entire life who ever truly listened."

My sister, **Sue Clement,** whose capacity to be empathetic, loving, and nonjudgmental (particularly when it comes to talking about our mother) is a precious gift.

My father, **Alan F. Kehr,** who taught me the virtues of striving to live an honorable life, the self-respect that comes from hard work, the pride that comes from lifelong learning, and that "you build your reputation over a lifetime and can lose it in a heartbeat."

Grandfather **Morris Louis Fuchs, MD**, a Hungarian immigrant who grew up desperately poor, living in a tenement in New York City, and who nonetheless served as a beloved family physician for over fifty-two years. His loving kindness with his patients inspired me to become a doctor.

Grandmother **Hilda Kehr**, a pioneer who "scandalized" our family in the 1920s by driving a car and teaching school ("proper ladies" didn't do such things back then), who was nationally honored for her work with the blind (she converted a physical chemistry textbook to Braille by hand so that a blind PhD candidate could continue her studies). Her unconditional love, grace, stature, and humility inspired me to serve others.

Grandfather **Abraham Kehr**, who left school in the eighth grade to support his family following the death of his father, survived a chemical-warfare attack as a soldier on the front lines in World War I, and went on to become a Golden Gloves champion and successful businessman. His determination in the face of overwhelming odds inspires me to constantly strive to test and exceed my limitations.

My editor **Becky Cabaza**, who patiently and persistently helped me find my voice.

Mary LoVerde, best-selling author and Hall of Fame speaker, whose friendship, cheerleading, and belief in me as a writer have been of inestimable value.

Child psychiatrist **Dr. John Meeks**, mentor, friend, and author of that famous book *The Fragile Alliance*, whose belief in me, and whose $5,000 in "venture capital," enabled me to start Potomac Psychiatry.

Dr. Izy Kogan, who survived the Holocaust and the many wars following Israel's partition, a brilliant physician and "brother," who is

242

always able to help put life in perspective, having lived through more history than anyone else I know. Thanks for the "tough love" too!

Dr. Michael Wannon, who taught me the values of curiosity, empathy, and emotional safety in all human relationships.

Dr. Mick Gill, who taught me how to enter the world of the most desperately ill patients, join them there to ease their aloneness, and assist their healthy Selves to develop a more powerful voice inside.

Dr. Ana-Marie Rizzuto, whose thoughtful, tender approach to fragile and vulnerable patients remains alive inside of me as I sit with those she taught me to treat.

Dr. Gerald Adler, who thankfully didn't bounce me out of the residency training program at Tufts New England Medical Center when, on my first weekend on call as a resident, I admitted a manic nineteen-year-old patient and placed him on lithium. My action created quite an angry stir among a number of his faculty members in the department, because no doctor at Tufts had ever prescribed it before. (I had learned about its use while studying at Maudsley and the Institute of Psychiatry in London the summer before).

Dr. Dan Buie, who taught me the value of compassion and humility while sitting with deeply disturbed patients and whose "there but for the grace of God go I" outlook remains a wellspring of gratitude inside me. I am also grateful for his comforting words when, convinced that Dr. Adler was going to fire me, Dan's first response was, "Bring me a couple of peer-reviewed journal articles on lithium, and I will go talk with Dr. Adler on your behalf."

Dr. Henry Friedman, who lambasted what he called "The Feelings Mafia" and taught me that most patients with borderline personality disorder first benefit from building ego strength, not exploring their feelings.

Dr. Elvin Semrad, residency group therapist, who began each interpretation with, "Is it true that . . . " As famous as he was, he taught us the value of *asking* rather than *telling* patients. Indirectly, he taught us about loss and grieving; he passed away during his tenure as our group leader. Ironically, he recorded each session with a machine called "Morpheus."

Dr. Hal Boris, the replacement group therapist, who once said, "Breasts and mouths, breasts and mouths. It is better to be in demand than demanding." This could be interpreted a number of different ways, but what I took from it is that it is better to become a source of emotional nourishment and strength for others rather than one who demands this from others. (Better to develop good ego strength.)

Dr. Elliot Schildkrout, our chief resident, whose humor often lifted our spirits as we first learned how to sit with patients suffering from unimaginable emotional pain.

The University of Pennsylvania and literature professors **Robert Lucid** and **John Edgar Wideman**, who profoundly influenced my understanding of human nature and taught me how to write about it.

Mr. James Giordano, my high-school English teacher, who had the audacity to teach us Existentialism in tenth grade at Abington High, forever altering my understanding of the human condition.

Harry Flemming, my "business psychiatrist," who generously provided "sessions" to surface and solve many of the emotional barriers that arise when growing a business.

Bill Wolfe, who taught me to "always hire the best talent." Even if you believe that you can't afford them, the return-on-investment will far outweigh the lower cost of mediocre talent.

My executive coach, **Tony Mayo**, and the band of "brother and sister executives" he assembled to help one another over the years. All of you have always been there for me and have taught me so much.

Jeff MacIntyre, CEO of Arimor, our digital marketing partner, whose enthusiasm for this entire project has been boundless and infectious.

Kat Fatland, my developmental editor at Greenleaf Book Group, who posed so many probing questions to me in the service of providing further clarity, continuity, and depth of experience for the reader and whose thoughtful, creative approach has made this book so very much stronger.

Nathan True, my lead editor at Greenleaf, who came up with the idea of converting the patient stories from narratives to dialogues, which has made them even more compelling and authentic.

Our entire Team at Greenleaf, whose enthusiasm, talent, high degree of professionalism, and belief in this book have provided me their personal brand of "healing sessions" for a somewhat stressed-out first author.

To friends with whom we've shared life's journey, who have always been there at times of joy and sorrow with boundless love and humor.

And finally, to my wonderful colleagues at Potomac Psychiatry, whose thirst for professional growth always keeps me on my toes and whose commitment to exceptional patient care remains a source of great pride.

APPENDIX

The Healing Companion™ Checklist

To accompany our sessions, I would like to teach you how to maintain an untangled heart and what to do if you develop emotional tangles once again. Here is a checklist of the key take-home messages from the sessions. If you're feeling stuck, review these points, and use your workbook as a reference as well.

You Are Not Alone

- ☑ Whenever you feel all tangled up inside, remember that there is always hope for you, no matter how desperate you feel.

- ☑ Every human heart is complicated and unsettled.

- ☑ Keep in mind these famous quotes: "Knowing yourself is the beginning of all wisdom," and "The unexamined life is not worth living."

- ☑ Whenever you begin to feel emotionally distressed, go back and review the relevant sections of your workbook that pertain to what you are feeling and the situation you find yourself in.

☑ Use the biopsychosocial model to analyze the possible causes of your emotional tangles, and ensure that the solutions you develop address any of the following domains that may apply:

- Your general health

- Possible side effects and drug interactions related to medications you are taking

- Developing and maintaining healthy brain function

- The unconscious and your early-childhood relationships

- Relationships at home, at work, and in your extended family

- Workplace stressors

- Your stage of life

- Existential issues (finding meaning and purpose)

- And, if applicable, your spiritual life

☑ Identify one or two people who you deeply trust, and be willing to talk with them at times of emotional upset and crisis. Allow them to touch you emotionally—and physically too, if that will give you more solace.

☑ Telling your story to someone you trust and being listened to with empathy and support go a long way toward helping you feel better.

☑ Listening to music can be emotionally therapeutic. It can bring comfort and ease your sense of aloneness.

Honest Self-Assessment

☑ Have the courage to face yourself and your problems.

☑ Routinely self-reflect. Remain aware of how you are thinking, feeling, and behaving toward others and how you are feeling about yourself. Consider taking ten or twenty minutes of uninterrupted time each evening to go into a quiet room and introspect about sources of distress in your life.

☑ Try not to run from painful or difficult feelings or to act out because of them. Allow these feelings to become conscious, learn how to tolerate them, and talk about them.

☑ Examine your childhood relationships with your parents to understand your current patterns of relating to your partner and your children.

☑ Be willing to learn about yourself by listening to what others have to say and thinking about whether their counsel may be right for you.

☑ What are the main patterns of thinking, feeling, and behaving that sabotage your life? What triggers these patterns, and how might you respond differently next time?

☑ Are there sources of learned helplessness or social defeat stress in your life? If so, how can you assert yourself to have more power over these sources or grow to need them less and begin to empower yourself or distance yourself from them?

☑ If you are a young adult going through an existential crisis, engage in therapy to help you learn how to express the true feelings that you have bottled up inside and to help you discover a new identity that feels right and true.

Don't Give Up

☑ If you are in psychotherapy with a therapist that you like and respect, stick with it, and bring up any and all feelings that you have about yourself, your loved ones, and the therapist.

☑ Continue in therapy until you have accomplished your goals for treatment. And when you feel ready to terminate, discuss your reasons with your therapist, and see whether the two of you can reach mutual agreement that it is time to end. Early termination may lead to a number of negative outcomes.

☑ Try not to feel ashamed of seeking treatment or taking medication (after all, you are suffering from a neurobiological condition), and ask for a detailed explanation for each and every medication that is prescribed.

Insist on Being Evaluated and Treated as a Whole Person

☑ Be mindful of how to select the right doctor or therapist. Choose someone who genuinely cares, who believes in you, and who creates a therapeutic relationship where you feel emotionally safe. Don't be afraid to seek a second opinion if your treatment is not going well. Use the selection criteria described in session 2 to make the right choice.

☑ Insist that your psychiatrist evaluate and treat your condition using the biopsychosocial model, and don't be afraid to advocate on your own behalf to achieve that gold standard: a full remission of symptoms.

☑ How might you be kinder and gentler to your brain? How are your behaviors (e.g., diet, alcohol or drugs, sedentary lifestyle) negatively affecting the functioning of this remarkable organ?

Relationships

☑ Search for a win–win solution in every relationship.

☑ Emotional intimacy and trust are difficult to establish and maintain. How do you sabotage intimacy in your most important relations?

☑ Do you repeatedly fall in love with narcissists or repeatedly bail on those who try to love you? How do your earliest childhood relationships influence how you think, feel, and behave toward your loved ones?

☑ Dissatisfaction is inevitable in every love relationship. Try to talk through the most important disappointments, and consider letting go of the less important ones.

☑ If your partner repeatedly neglects or abuses you, and if they refuse all of your efforts to engage in a dialogue to improve the relationship, seek out enough emotional support and inner strength to leave. You deserve emotional safety and a happier life.

☑ Any enduring love relationship will need to evolve through three phases: the romanticized phase, the reality phase, and the durable reality phase. It is impossible to remain in the romanticized phase indefinitely.

☑ Every real relationship has its ups and downs. For a loving bond to endure over time, you must develop a realistic perspective on what is possible, as opposed to fantasies (based on movies and romance novels) and unrealistic wishes and demands. Work within yourself and with your partner to develop mature adult love for one another.

☑ Create an atmosphere of emotional and physical safety.

☑ Trust is fragile, difficult to develop and maintain, and easy to damage or destroy. Strive not to betray the trust that your partner has placed in you.

☑ Loving feelings may also be fragile and may seem to evaporate if chronic feelings of anger, sadness, and disappointment develop. Your love for them may still be there, buried under many other feelings. The opposite of love is not hate; it is indifference.

☑ Anger can be a smokescreen under which many other feelings lie, such as sadness, disappointment, loneliness, humiliation, guilt, shame, regret, and even love. It is important to recognize and talk about all of these feelings. It is difficult for anyone to approach or get close to an angry partner. Empathy, compassion, and closeness become far more likely when a partner openly shares the feelings underneath the anger.

☑ Expect that emotional and sexual intimacy stir up deeply felt and largely unconscious conflicts and fantasies around dependence and independence, loyalty and betrayal, respect and disrespect, need satisfaction and disappointment, commitment and fears of abandonment, trust and mistrust, narcissistic love and mature love, and freedom and self-sacrifice. These conflicts originate in our earliest relationships with our parents and may be magnified by later love relations. Be willing to explore, understand, and resolve these conflicts, as opposed to acting out in ways that destroy intimate bonds.

☑ If your love relationship is in trouble, reconstruct where it first went off track and what you and your partner were independently living through at that time. Be willing to talk about your insights with them.

☑ Develop a gratitude list and add to it frequently—daily, if possible.

☑ Be willing to be the first to apologize after a fight, and mean it when you commit to changing behaviors that drive your partner away.

☑ Insist on being treated with respect by your partner. If you are not treated with respect, you won't be able to feel self-respect.

☑ Listen from your heart with empathy and curiosity. Pay attention without interrupting. Work hard to understand what you are being told and communicate your understanding, even if you don't agree with what is being said or find it offensive.

☑ Put yourself in your partner's place.

☑ Listen to your partner with a spirit of cooperation, and jointly embark on a journey of discovery and mutual need satisfaction.

☑ Demonstrate and be grateful for small acts of love. These can reverse a destructive downward spiral and bring much-needed hope.

☑ Avoid entering into a love relationship with a narcissist who lacks any capacity for empathy and compassion and is unwilling to listen to and respect your feelings.

☑ If you are already in a committed relationship with a narcissist, or have not achieved a mature love relationship, use the techniques I outlined in sessions 7 and 8 to improve the relationship, and if your partner refuses to participate, work on securing enough emotional support to get out.

Responsibility and Empathy

☑ Remaining angry and entitled and consistently blaming others is a great recipe for a tangled heart.

☑ Strive to lead a virtuous life, and "walk the talk" with your children, other loved ones, and colleagues.

☑ Recognize that each and every person in your life is someone who has their own hopes, dreams, fears, goals, and emotional conflicts—that it is not just about you; it is also about them.

☑ Try to listen to others with empathy and curiosity. You don't need to agree with their point of view to listen, learn, and offer compassion.

For Parents

☑ Enter your child's world, listen, provide empathy and kindness, and treat them with respect, even when you disagree with their point of view.

☑ At the same time, reassure your child that you understand and respect their need for privacy.

☑ Be there to help your child over the hurdles in life that they can't overcome by themselves. Try not to rush in and rescue them from situations they can manage on their own, and encourage them to take on and master challenging situations, to gain wisdom and become more resilient.

☑ Communicate directly that you understand your child's perspective (while not necessarily agreeing with it). Remember what it felt like when you were their age. How would you have wanted to be treated by your parents?

☑ Be willing to share with them some of the mistakes that you made when you were growing up and how you overcame them.

☑ Reward respectful behavior toward you with affection, pride, and praise.

☑ Rather than force your passions on your child (to satisfy your own narcissistic needs), encourage them to discover and explore their own passions, and when these change (and they inevitably will), be supportive.

☑ Challenge your child to persist in the face of adversity and provide support when the going gets tough, without being judgmental if they complain about how hard it is. Be encouraging instead, and let them know that you feel proud of their efforts to hang in there.

☑ Don't be afraid to teach the values illustrated in *The Book of Virtues*, and be certain that you exemplify them in your own life, if you wish your child to adopt them.

☑ If your child sustains a deeply humiliating experience, provide empathetic parental support and encouragement to overcome and master their feelings of fear, and help restore positive self-esteem. Avoid reacting in anger out of your own feelings of helplessness.

☑ If your child has been sexually or physically abused, seek out professional help as soon as possible to reduce immediate and long-term damage.

☑ If you are the parent of a young adult that may be going through an existential crisis,

- Insist that your child seek professional help.

- Learn how (with help from the therapist) to encourage your child to talk about and reveal their true feelings and self, without judging them.

- Reassure them that you will still love them even if they decide to embark on a very different path from before.

- Get emotional support to help you cope with your feelings of shock and helplessness.

- Encourage your child to work with their therapist to figure out an identity that is truer to their core personality, and provide compassionate support during what will likely be a torturous process over several years.

- Make certain that ADHD and a major mood disorder are considered by the doctor in the diagnostic evaluation and that incapacitating symptoms are treated with medication.

The Empty Nest

☑ It is a bittersweet time and raises many issues related to your life stage, such as the end of an era and your mortality. Be mindful of these feelings, and share them with your partner or a trusted friend, as opposed to acting on them.

☑ Make your partner feel that they are number one in your life.

☑ Consult together around thorny issues in raising your child.

☑ Have weekly date nights, and share some weekends or vacations, just the two of you (no kids invited!).

☑ Periodically check in with your partner to see how they are feeling about themselves and life in general.

☑ Find ways to provide emotional support to one another when challenged as parents and with respect to other sources of stress in your busy lives.

☑ Share in pursuits that you both find pleasurable and meaningful.

☑ Although you may no longer feel love toward your partner, those feelings may still be inside you. Perhaps they are buried beneath years of disappointment, anger, sadness, and other feelings. Talking through these issues may allow you to rediscover your love.

☑ Actively focus on and discuss your relationship with your partner.

☑ Look hard at yourself in the mirror, and acknowledge that you are facing life stage issues that can feel daunting. Identify and talk about them with someone to get emotional support.

☑ Think about ways that you and your partner can better support each other as you are growing older.

☑ Share with each other your feelings about this bittersweet time.

☑ Engage in the process of reinventing an emotional connection with one another, and work hard to rediscover your friendship.

☑ Reminisce with one another about the good times you shared.

☑ Talk about rediscovering activities that you both enjoyed once upon a time.

☑ A better emotional connection, and ensuring emotional safety, will often rekindle sexual intimacy.

☑ Seek couples or individual therapy if you remain stuck in an unhappy place.

☑ If you work through some of these thorny issues, the empty nest stage of life can bring about a newfound sense of freedom and the opportunity to get out and explore the world unencumbered by children!

For Survivors of Abuse

☑ If you were subjected to childhood neglect or abuse, seek professional help. You don't have to live the rest of your life feeling like "damaged goods." You deserve to recover from these traumas and to find emotional intimacy, love, and trust with another.

☑ Developing trust and emotional intimacy with another human being will be challenging.

☑ Feeling emotionally safe with your romantic partner may seem impossible.

☑ The perpetrator of the abuse may have once been a trusted and caring relation in your life, who abused their position of trust to prey on you.

☑ Out of a wish to please them, to satisfy your unmet emotional needs for love and affection, and because of your naïveté and confusion (after all, you were just a child), you were manipulated and willingly consented, resulting in intense feelings of guilt and shame. Children who are molested inherently follow the lead of what "big people" (adults) ask them to do, even if the adult is a stranger. The responsibility for what happened belongs with the adult, not with you.

☑ When initially solicited, you may have felt quite special, even adored, yet those feelings will give way to deeply painful, confusing, and contradictory feelings. As a result, you developed extensive damage to your emerging self, psychosexual development, and self-esteem.

☑ The emotional damage resulting from the trauma can create a pattern of troubled relationships with lovers and within yourself, as well as deeply held fears that your own child will be victimized.

☑ Face what was done to you, as opposed to running away from the memories and feelings. This can be done through introspection, journaling, speaking with a loved one or friend who is caring and empathetic, and psychotherapy.

☑ Have the courage to enter into a psychoanalytic psychotherapy, prolonged exposure therapy, or psychoanalysis.

☑ Choosing the right therapist for you is crucial. It takes a great deal of courage to face yourself, what was done to you, the feelings that it engendered, and your horror over it all. You want to select someone who is really talented. Use the selection criteria described in session 2 to make the right choice.

☑ Choose a therapist you come to feel emotionally safe with as the relationship develops (recall the concept of the *safe base* of childhood) and who is experienced in treating trauma survivors.

☑ The feelings that you once experienced and repressed into your unconscious mind may be so intense and frightening that they feel unmanageable, including powerful feelings of shame, humiliation, and rage that mutilated your self-esteem.

☑ There is a horror you may experience that extends to many of the feelings and memories that return as you explore what was done to you in talk therapy. Horror may develop over rage-filled and sadistic feelings and fantasies, including wanting to torture and destroy those responsible for the abuse (including sadistic sexual fantasies), abolish the place where it happened, and eradicate all of the memories associated with the horrid experience.

☑ As a result, the therapeutic alliance with your therapist may be challenged during the course of treatment as you experience impulses to avoid disturbing feelings, miss sessions, evade painful sessions filled with sobbing and self-loathing, and drop out of therapy altogether.

☑ The work in therapy is long and painstaking but immensely rewarding if you see it through. It enables you to begin to trust in your loved ones and open yourself up to the possibility of fully loving and being loved.

☑ It may well be a long road before you are able to heal yourself, and it can feel scary and daunting along the way. Feel hopeful, remain optimistic, and stick with it.

Notes

Session 1

1. Kendra Cherry, "What Is the Unconscious?" *verywell*, last modified May 30, 2016, https://www.verywell.com/what-is-the-unconscious-2796004.

2. *Encyclopeædia Britannica Online*, s. v. "Repression," last modified April 21, 2009, https://www.britannica.com/topic/repression-psychology.

3. Jane Milton, "What is Psychoanalytic Psychotherapy?" *British Psychoanalytic Council*, last modified 2014, accessed August 26, 2016, http://www.bpc.org.uk/about-psychotherapy/what-psychotherapy.

4. The Free Dictionary, s. v. "Transference (psychology)," accessed August 26, 2016, http://medical-dictionary.thefreedictionary.com/Transference+(psychology).

5. Kendra Cherry, "What Is Psychotherapy?" *verywell*, last modified May 9, 2016, http://psychology.about.com/od/psychotherapy/a/what-is-psychotherapy.htm.

6. Thomas L. Schwartz, "Psychopharmacology Today: Where Are We and Where Do We Go from Here?" *Mens Sana Monograph* 8 (2010): 6–16, doi:10.4103/0973-1229.58816, http://www.ncbi.nlm.nih.gov/pmc/articles/PMC3031936/.
   "Stahl Online," Cambridge University Press, accessed August 26, 2016, http://stahlonline.cambridge.org/.
   Thomas L. Schwartz, "Introduction: Looking to the Future of Psychopharmacology," *Psychiatric Times*, April 19, 2011, http://www.psychiatrictimes.com/articles/introduction-looking-future-psychopharmacology.

7. Francesc Borrell-Carrió, Anthony L. Suchman, and Ronald M. Epstein, "The Biopsychosocial Model 25 Years Later: Principles, Practice, and

Scientific Inquiry," *Annals of Family Medicine* 2 (2004): 576–582, http://www.ncbi.nlm.nih.gov/pmc/articles/PMC1466742/.

8. Bob Weinhold, "Epigenetics: The Science of Change," *Environmental Health Perspectives* 114 (2006): A160–A167, http://www.ncbi.nlm.nih.gov/pmc/articles/PMC1392256/.
Jorge Alejandro Alegría-Torres, Andrea Baccarelli, and Valentina Bollati, "Epigenetics and Lifestyle," *Epigenomics* 3 (2011): 267–277, http://www.ncbi.nlm.nih.gov/pmc/articles/PMC3752894/.

9. James P. Hamilton, "Epigenetics: Principles and Practice," *Digestive Diseases* 29 (2011): 130–135, https://www.ncbi.nlm.nih.gov/pmc/articles/PMC3134032.
Bhavya Ravi and Manoj Kannan, "Epigenetics in the Nervous System: An Overview of Its Essential Role," *Indian Journal of Human Genetics* 19 (2013): 384–391, https://www.ncbi.nlm.nih.gov/pmc/articles/PMC3897130.

10. As discussed in an article in *Psychology Today* about the field of Music Therapy and the music-emotion connection (http://www.psychologytoday.com/blog/your-musical-self/201311/music-your-gps-voice-and-the-science-timbre), the music-emotion connection is one of the primary mechanisms underlying why music therapy works. Music therapists learn to manipulate timbre as a way to connect with clients, influence them emotionally, grab their attention, and help them sustain their focus. Timbre itself can help build and release tension, and it can impact emotional expressions and perceptions. Thus, the compositions linked to in each session may have a beneficial therapeutic effect on you.
Kimberly Sena Moore, "Music, Your GPS Voice, and the Science of Timbre," *Psychology Today*, November 1, 2013, http://www.psychologytoday.com/blog/your-musical-self/201311/music-your-gps-voice-and-the-science-timbre.
Kimberly Sena Moore, "Top 12 Reasons Why I Have a Job: Why Music Therapy Works," *Psychology Today*, June 7, 2010, https://www.psychologytoday.com/blog/your-musical-self/201006/top-12-reasons-why-i-have-job.

11. Lawrence Greenman, "Neuroscience and Psychoanalysis: Approaches to Consciousness and Thinking," *Psychiatry* 4 (2007): 51–57, https://www.ncbi.nlm.nih.gov/pmc/articles/PMC2921242.
Saul McLeod, "Unconscious Mind," *Simply Psychology* (2015), http://www.simplypsychology.org/unconscious-mind.html.
Reference.com, "What Is Sigmund Freud's Iceberg Theory?" Reference.com website, https://www.reference.com/world-view/sigmund-freud-s-iceberg-theory-befcbf1fb28c1d50#.

Session 2

1. Kristi A. DeName, "Repetition Compulsion: Why Do We Repeat the Past?" *World of Psychology* (blog), *PsychCentral*, last modified August 6, 2015, http://psychcentral.com/blog/archives/2013/06/29/repetition-compulsion-why-do-we-repeat-the-past/.

2. D. W. Winnicott, *The Maturational Processes and the Facilitating Environment: Studies in the Theory of Emotional Development* (London: The International Psycho-Analytical Press, 1965), http://www.abebe.org.br/wp-content/uploads/Donald-Winnicott-The-Maturational-Process-and-the-Facilitating-Environment-Studies-in-the-Theory-of-Emotional-Development-1965.pdf.
Good Therapy, "Donald Winnicott (1896–1971)," GoodTherapy.com website (2015), http://www.goodtherapy.org/famous-psychologists/donald-winnicott.html.

3. Bennett Pologne, "Resistance," About Psychotherapy, accessed August 26, 2016, http://www.aboutpsychotherapy.com/Tresistance.php.

4. "Transference," Psychoanalysis, accessed August 26, 2016, http://www.freudfile.org/psychoanalysis/transference.html.

5. Steven Reidbord, "Countertransference, an Overview: What is Countertransference?" *Psychology Today*, March 24, 2010, https://www.psychologytoday.com/blog/sacramento-street-psychiatry/201003/countertransference-overview.

6. J. Jones, "About the Free Associations Method," trans. Mihaela Cristea, *Psychoanalysis: Techniques and Practice*, accessed August 26, 2016, http://www.freudfile.org/psychoanalysis/free_associations.html.
Jane Milton, "What is Psychoanalytic Psychotherapy?" *British Psychoanalytic Council*, last modified 2014, http://www.bpc.org.uk/about-psychotherapy/what-psychotherapy.

7. Renée Grinnell, "Abreaction," *PsychCentral*, last modified July 17, 2016, http://psychcentral.com/encyclopedia/abreaction/.
"Abreaction," Freudscases wiki, accessed August 26, 2016, http://freudscases.wikispaces.com/Abreaction.

8. Göran Högberg, Davide Nardo, Tore Hällström, and Marco Pagani, "Affective Psychotherapy in Post-Traumatic Reactions Guided by Affective Neuroscience: Memory Reconsolidation and Play," *Psychology Research and Behavior Management* 4 (2011): 87–96, doi:10.2147/PRBM.S10380, http://www.ncbi.nlm.nih.gov/pmc/articles/PMC3218787/.

9. Marna S. Barrett, Wee-Jhong Chua, Paul Crits-Cristoph, Mary Beth

Gibbons, D. Casiano, and Don Thompson, "Early Withdrawal from Mental Health Treatment: Implications for Psychotherapy Practice," *Psychotherapy* 45 (2008): 247–267, doi:10.1037/00333204.45.2.247, http://www.ncbi.nlm.nih.gov/pmc/articles/PMC2762228/.

Lisa Wallner Samstag, Sarai T. Batchelder, J. Cristopher Muran, Jeremy D. Safran, and Arnold Winston, "Early Identification of Treatment Failures in Short-Term Psychotherapy: An Assessment of Therapeutic Alliance and Interpersonal Behavior," *The Journal of Psychotherapy Practice and Research* 7 (1998): 126–143, http://www.ncbi.nlm.nih.gov/pmc/articles/PMC3330493/.

Session 3

1. Albert Ellis, Mike Abrams, and Lidia Abrams, *Personality Theories: Critical Perspectives* (Los Angeles: Sage, 2009), 452, https://books.google.com/books?id=OObiJhzBtpMC&pg=PA452&lpg=PA452&dq=first+separation+individuation+object+relations&source=bl&ots=eRkkeMmvDT&sig=4OTFl5rHj5zuaZFoMaGULJSHm0I&hl=en&sa=X&ved=0CFMQ6AEwCWoVChMIwYHJhqiixwIVAmg-Ch3cIAvk#v=onepage&q=first%20separation%20individuation%20object%20relations&f=false.

2. Jamie McLean, "Psychotherapy with a Narcissistic Patient Using Kohut's Self Psychology Model," *Psychiatry* 4 (2007): 40–47, http://www.ncbi.nlm.nih.gov/pmc/articles/PMC2860525/.

3. If you would like some formal guidance in this process at work, consider exploring The Birkman Method: https://www.youtube.com/watch?v=gwXVCB1YGY8. See also https://www.birkman.com/news/view/the-birkman-method-your-personality-at-work.

4. Angela Lee Duckworth, "Grit: The Power of Passion and Perseverance," filmed April 2013, TED video, posted May 2013, http://www.ted.com/talks/angela_lee_duckworth_grit_the_power_of_passion_and_perseverance.

5. Jay Belsky, "Rewards Are Better than Punishment: Here's Why," *Psychology Today*, September 2008, https://www.psychologytoday.com/blog/family-affair/200809/rewards-are-better-punishment-here-s-why.

6. Canadian Pædiatric Society, "Effective Discipline for Children," *Pædiatrics and Child Health* 9 (2004): 37–41, http://www.ncbi.nlm.nih.gov/pmc/articles/PMC2719514/.

Session 4

1. Christopher L. Heffner, "Erikson's Stages of Psychosocial Development," in *Psychology 101* (AllPsych, 2001), http://allpsych.com/psychology101/social_development/.

2. Denis Mellier, "The Psychic Envelopes in Psychoanalytic Theory of Infancy," *Frontiers in Psychology* 5 (2014): 734, doi:10.3389/fpsyg.2014.00734, http://journal.frontiersin.org/article/10.3389/fpsyg.2014.00734/abstract.

3. Debra Kaminer, Soraya Seedat, and Dan J. Stein, "Post-traumatic Stress Disorder in Children," *World Psychiatry* 4 (2005): 121–125, https://www.ncbi.nlm.nih.gov/pmc/articles/PMC1414752.

4. "Stress Management," Mayo Clinic, May 8, 2014, http://www.mayoclinic.org/healthy-lifestyle/stress-management/in-depth/relaxation-technique/art-20045368?pg=2.

5. Johanna S. Kaplan, "Exposure Therapy for Anxiety Disorders," *Psychiatric Times*, September 6, 2011, http://www.psychiatrictimes.com/anxiety/exposure-therapy-anxiety-disorders.

Session 5

1. Joseph Walsh and Jim Lantz, "The Nature of Existential Crisis," in *Short-Term Existential Intervention in Clinical Practice* (Chicago: Lyceum Books, 2007), 1–12, http://www.lyceumbooks.com/pdf/ShortTermExistential_Chapter_01.pdf.

2. D.W. Winnicott, "Ego Distortion in Terms of True and False Self," in *The Maturational Process and the Facilitating Environment: Studies in the Theory of Emotional Development* (London: Hogarth Press, 1965), 140–152, https://s3.amazonaws.com/arena-attachments/665041/698755275e4db3e78bf88dd7e0a0beea.pdf.

3. Rita B. Ardito and Daniela Rabellino, "Therapeutic Alliance and Outcome of Psychotherapy: Historical Excursus, Measurements, and Prospects for Research," *Frontiers in Psychology* 2 (2011): 270, doi:10.3389/fpsyg.2011.00270, http://www.ncbi.nlm.nih.gov/pmc/articles/PMC3198542/.
    Alain De Mijolia, "Therapeutic Alliance," *International Dictionary of Psychoanalysis*, Encyclopedia.com, 2005, http://www.encyclopedia.com/doc/1G2-3435301472.html.

Session 6

1. Margaret Crastnopol, "Older Adolescents with Academic Achievement Problems," in *Psychotherapies with Children and Adolescents* (Washington, DC: American Psychiatric Press, 1992), 238, https://books.google.com/books?id=YNgFXK1dHS4C&pg=PA238&lpg=PA238&dq=discussion+of+the+fragile+alliance+treating+adolescents&source=bl&ots=Kk8ZBODkWN&sig=6qy0fPXxHKlyqrT4Jgdp8FOyF5M&hl=en&sa=X&ved=0CFIQ6AEwCGoVChMInoDKx9fOxwIVy3E-Ch2tdQM-#v=onepage&q=discussion%20of%20the%20fragile%20alliance%20treating%20adolescents&f=false.

Session 7

1. Consider the example of Wesley and Buttercup in that wonderful movie about true love, *The Princess Bride*.

2. The movie *Beginners* beautifully and poignantly addresses some of these issues.

3. Lisa Firestone, "4 Ways You Could Be Sabotaging Your Relationship," *Psychology Today*, January 5, 2015, https://www.psychologytoday.com/blog/compassion-matters/201501/4-ways-you-could-be-sabotaging-your-relationship.

4. Lisa Firestone, "One Surprising Reason We Sabotage Love," *Psychology Today*, May 26, 2014, https://www.psychologytoday.com/blog/compassion-matters/201405/one-surprising-reason-we-sabotage-love.

5. S. W. Jackson, "Catharsis and Abreaction in the History of Psychological Healing," *Psychiatric Clinics of North America* 17 (1994): 471–491, http://www.ncbi.nlm.nih.gov/pubmed/7824376.

6. L. E. Brumariu and K. A. Kerns, "Parent–Child Attachment and Internalizing Symptoms in Childhood and Adolescence: A Review of Empirical Findings and Future Directions," *Development and Psychopathology* 22 (2010): 177–203, doi:10.1017/S0954579409990344, http://www.ncbi.nlm.nih.gov/pubmed/20102655.

7. Mayo Clinic Staff, "Narcissistic Personality Disorder," Mayo Clinic website (2014), http://www.mayoclinic.com/health/narcissistic-personality-disorder/DS00652/DSECTION=symptoms.

Session 8

1. John A. Bargh and Ezequiel Morsella, "The Unconscious Mind," *Perspectives on Psychological Science* 3 (2008): 73–79, doi:10.1111/j.1745-6916.2008.00064.x, http://www.ncbi.nlm.nih.gov/pmc/articles/PMC2440575/.

Session 10

1. Stephen A. Diamond, "Essential Secrets of Psychotherapy: Repetitive Relationship Patterns," *Psychology Today*, June 14, 2008, https://www.psychologytoday.com/blog/evil-deeds/200806/essential-secrets-psychotherapy-repetitive-relationship-patterns.

2. Renée Grinnell, "Abreaction," *PsychCentral*, last modified July 17, 2016, http://psychcentral.com/encyclopedia/abreaction/.

3. Andrea Mathews, "Acting Out: Learning to Hold the Tension," *Psychology Today*, April 29, 2012, https://www.psychologytoday.com/blog/traversing-the-inner-terrain/201204/acting-out.

4. "Facts and Statistics," The US Department of Justice, National Sex Offender Public Website, accessed August 26, 2016, https://www.nsopw.gov/en-US/Education/FactsStatistics?AspxAutoDetectCookieSupport=1. "Child Sexual Abuse Statics," Darkness to Light, accessed August 26, 2016, http://www.d2l.org/atf/cf/%7B64AF78C4-5EB8-45AA-BC28-F7EE2B581919%7D/all_statistics_20150619.pdf.

5. Jorge Alejandro Alegría-Torres, Andrea Baccarelli, and Valentina Bollati, "Epigenetics and Lifestyle," *Epigenomics* 3 (2011): 267–277, https://www.ncbi.nlm.nih.gov/pmc/articles/PMC3752894.

6. Edward E. Smith and Stephen M. Kosslyn, eds., *Cognitive Psychology: Mind and Brain*, (London: Pearson, 2006), http://www-psych.stanford.edu/~ashas/Cognition%20Textbook/chapter6.pdf.

7. Parris M. Kidd, "Omega-3 DHA and EPA for Cognition, Behavior, and Mood: Clinical Findings and Structural-Functional Synergies with Cell Membrane Phospholipids," *Alternative Medicine Review* 12 (2007): 207–227, http://www.ncbi.nlm.nih.gov/pubmed/18072818.

8. R. Chris Fraley, "A Brief Overview of Adult Attachment Theory and Research," R. Chris Fraley website, University of Illinois at Urbana-Champaign Psychology Department Member Resources, accessed August 2, 2016, https://internal.psychology.illinois.edu/~rcfraley/attachment.htm.

9. "What is DBT?" The Linehan Institute Behavioral Tech Research, accessed August 26, 2016, http://behavioraltech.org/resources/whatisdbt.cfm.

10. Sarah Knox, Julie L. Goldberg, Susan S. Woodhouse, and Clara E. Hill, "Clients' Internal Representations of Their Therapists," *Journal of Counseling Psychology* 46 (1999): 244–256, http://epublications.marquette.edu/cgi/viewcontent.cgi?article=1013&context=edu_fac.

Session 11

1. Beth E. Molnar, Stephen L. Buka, and Ronald C. Kessler, "Child Sexual Abuse and Subsequent Psychopathology: Results from the National Comorbidity Survey," *American Journal of Public Health* 91 (2001): 753–760, http://www.ncbi.nlm.nih.gov/pmc/articles/PMC1446666/pdf/11344883.pdf.
B. E. Molnar, L. F. Berkman, and S. L. Buka, "Psychopathology, Childhood Sexual Abuse and Other Childhood Adversities: Relative Links to Subsequent Suicidal Behaviour in the US," *Psychological Medicine* 31 (2001): 965–977, doi:10.1017/S0033291701004329, http://www.ncbi.nlm.nih.gov/pubmed/11513382.

2. Megan Spokas, Amy Wenzel, Shannon Wiltsey Stirman, Gregory K. Brown, and Aaron T. Beck, "Suicide Risk Factors and Mediators Between Childhood Sexual Abuse and Suicide Ideation Among Male and Female Suicide Attempters," *Journal of Traumatic Stress* 22 (2009): 467–470, doi:10.1002/jts.20438, http://www.ncbi.nlm.nih.gov/pmc/articles/PMC2767398/.

3. Susan Krauss Whitbourne, "The One Emotion that Really Hurts Your Brain," *Psychology Today*, July 9, 2014, https://www.psychologytoday.com/blog/fulfillment-any-age/201407/the-one-emotion-really-hurts-your-brain.
A. E. Farmer and P. McGussin, "Humiliation, Loss and Other Types of Life Events and Difficulties: A Comparison of Depressed Subjects, Healthy Controls and Their Siblings," *Psychological Medicine* 33 (2003): 1169–1175, doi:10.1017/S0033291703008419, http://www.ncbi.nlm.nih.gov/pubmed/14580071.
A. Collazzoni, C. Capanna, M. Bustini, C. Marucci, S. Prescenzo, M. Ragusa, A. Tosone, V. Di Ubaldo, P. Stratta, and A. Rossi, "A Comparison of Humiliation Measurement in a Depressive Versus Non-Clinical Sample: A Possible Clinical Utility," *Journal of Clinical Psychology* 71 (2015): 1218–1224, doi:10.1002/jclp.22212, http://www.ncbi.nlm.nih.gov/pubmed/26275166.

M. Otten and K. J. Jonas, "Humiliation as an Intense Emotional Experience: Evidence from the Electro-Encephalogram," *Social Neuroscience* 9 (2013), doi:10.1080/17470919.2013.855660, http://www.ncbi.nlm.nih.gov/pubmed/24215103.

4. Ketevan Glonti, Vladimir S. Gordeev, Yeveniy Goryakin, Aaron Reeves, David Stuckler, Martin McKee, and Bayard Roberts, "A Systematic Review on Health Resilience to Economic Crises," *PLoS One* 10 (2015), doi:10.1371/journal.pone.0123117, http://www.ncbi.nlm.nih.gov/pmc/articles/PMC4408106/.
   Office of the Surgeon General (US), *2012 National Strategy for Suicide Prevention* (Washington, DC: US Department of Health & Human Services, 2012), http://www.ncbi.nlm.nih.gov/books/NBK109906/.

5. "Transference," Psychoanalysis, accessed August 26, 2016, http://www.freudfile.org/psychoanalysis/transference.html.

6. Leonard Shengold, *Soul Murder Revisited: Thoughts about Therapy, Hate, Love, and Memory* (New Haven, CT: Yale University Press, 2000), https://www.nytimes.com/books/first/s/shengold-soul.html.

7. Gregg Henriques, "One Self or Many Selves?" *Psychology Today*, April 25, 2014, https://www.psychologytoday.com/blog/theory-knowledge/201404/one-self-or-many-selves.
   David Spiegel, "Coming Apart: Trauma and the Fragmentation of the Self," *Cerebrum*, January 31, 2008, http://www.dana.org/Cerebrum/2008/Coming_Apart__Trauma_and_the_Fragmentation_of_the_Self/.

8. "Emotional Defenses," Order of Saint Patrick website, last modified April 9, 2015, http://orderofsaintpatrick.org/relations/defenses.htm.

9. James A. Chu, Lisa M. Frey, Barbara L. Ganzel, and Julia A. Matthews, "Memories of Childhood Abuse: Dissociation, Amnesia, and Corroboration," *American Journal of Psychiatry* 156 (1999): 749–755, doi:10.1176/ajp.156.5.749, http://ajp.psychiatryonline.org/doi/10.1176/ajp.156.5.749.

10. Göran Högberg, Davide Nardo, Tore Hällström, and Marco Pagani, "Affective Psychotherapy in Post-Traumatic Reactions Guided by Affective Neuroscience: Memory Reconsolidation and Play," *Psychology Research and Behavior Management* 4 (2011): 87–96, doi:10.2147/PRBM.S10380, http://www.ncbi.nlm.nih.gov/pmc/articles/PMC3218787/.

11. John Bowlby, "The Nature of the Child's Tie to His Mother," *International Journal of Psycho-Analysis* 39 (1958): 350–373, http://www.psychology.sunysb.edu/attachment/online/nature%20of%20the%20childs%20tie%20bowlby.pdf.

12. Christine Walsh, Harriet L. MacMillan, and Ellen Jamieson, "The Relationship Between Parental Substance Abuse and Child Maltreatment: Findings from the Ontario Health Supplement," *Child Abuse and Neglect* 27 (2003): 1409–1425, doi:10.1016/j. chiabu.2003.07.002, http://www.ncbi.nlm.nih.gov/pubmed/14644058. Sam Choi and Gail Tittle, "Parental Substance Abuse and Child Maltreatment Literature Review," Children and Family Research Center, May 2002, http://cfrc.illinois.edu/pubs/lr_20020501_ ParentalSubstanceAbuseAndChildMaltreatment.pdf. Aaron M. White, David W. Jamieson-Drake, H. Scott Swartzwelder, "Prevalence and Correlates of Alcohol-Induced Blackouts Among College Students: Results of an E-Mail Survey," *Journal of American College Health* 51 (2002): 117–131, doi:10.1080/07448480209596339, http://www.ncbi.nlm.nih.gov/pubmed/12638993. Shanta R. Dube, Robert F. Anda, Vincent J. Felitti, Janet B. Croft, Valerie J. Edwards, and Wayne H. Giles, "Growing Up with Parental Alcohol Abuse: Exposure to Childhood Abuse, Neglect, and Household Dysfunction," *Child Abuse & Neglect* 25 (2001): 1627–1640, doi:10.1016/S0145-2134(01)00293-9, http://www.ncbi.nlm.nih.gov/ pubmed/11814159.

13. Jody Davies and Mary Gail Frawley, *Treating the Adult Survivor of Childhood Sexual Abuse* (New York: Basic Books, 1994), 167–185, https://manhattanpsychoanalysis.com/wp-content/uploads/readings/ Mandelbaum_course/Treating%20Adult%20Survivor%20of%20 Childhood%20Sexual%20Abuse-Davies%20&%20Frawley.pdf. C. J. Dalenberg, *Countertransference and the Treatment of Trauma* (Washington, DC: American Psychological Association, 2000), http:// psycnet.apa.org/books/10380. Deborah Spermon, Yvonne Darlington, and Paul Gibney, "Psychodynamic Psychotherapy for Complex Trauma: Targets, Focus, Applications, and Outcomes," *Psychology Research and Behavior Management* 3 (2010): 119–127, http://www.ncbi.nlm.nih.gov/pmc/articles/PMC3218759/#b33 -prbm-3-119. Michelle Price, "Incest: Transference and Countertransference Implications," *Journal of the American Academy of Psychoanalysis and Dynamic Psychiatry* 22 (1994): 211–229, http://www.ncbi.nlm.nih.gov/ pubmed/7961039.

14. "Adult Survivors of Childhood Sexual Abuse," RAINN, accessed August 26, 2016, https://www.rainn.org/get-info/effects-of-sexual-assault/ adult-survivors-of-childhood-sexual-abuse.

15. Karen A. Olio and William F. Cornell, "The Therapeutic Relationship as the Foundation for Treatment with Adult Survivors of Sexual Abuse," *Psychotherapy: Theory, Research, Practice, Training* 30 (1993): 512–523, http://kspope.com/memory/relationship.php.
Elisabeth Cronin, Bethany L. Brand, and Jonathan F. Mattanah, "The Impact of the Therapeutic Alliance on Treatment Outcome in Patients with Dissociative Disorders," *European Journal of Psychotraumatology* 5 (2014), doi:10.3402/ejpt.v5.22676, http://www.ncbi.nlm.nih.gov/pmc/articles/PMC3946510/.

Index

D

About the Author

Author and national award-winning psychiatrist Bruce Alan Kehr, MD, is the founder and president of Potomac Psychiatry (PotomacPsychiatry.com) since 1981. *Washingtonian* magazine awarded him their Top Doctor designation from 2012 to 2017. In 2016, the magazine named him The Face of Psychiatry in their "Faces of Washington" issue. Dr. Kehr serves on the Board of the Institute on Aging of the University of Pennsylvania and served as its chairman from 2006 to 2009. The readers and editors of *PharmaVOICE* selected him in 2007 as one of the 100 Most Inspiring and Influential Leaders in the Life Sciences Industry. He is also an Eagle Scout.

Dr. Kehr received training in psychiatry at Tufts New England Medical Center, where he was chief resident; in neuropsychiatry at the VA Boston Healthcare System—Jamaica Plain; and in psychoanalysis at the Boston Psychoanalytic Institute. He practices psychiatry and psychotherapy using the biopsychosocial model, designed to evaluate and treat the whole person by understanding each individual's unique genetic, biological, psychological, social, and life-stage attributes.

Author photo by Michael Bennett Kress Photography.

Dr. Kehr lives in Potomac, Maryland, with his wife, Barbara, a psychotherapist. They have two daughters: Melanie, an immigration attorney who advocates for asylum on behalf of refugees fleeing domestic violence and child abuse, and Lisa, a psychiatric nurse practitioner graduate student.

Learn more by visiting DrBruceKehr.com.